Mr Talbott
with affectionate
regards –
W. G. – Duffield

MISREAD PASSAGES

OF

SCRIPTURE.

BY

J. BALDWIN BROWN, B.A.,

Author of "The Divine Life in Man," "The Home Life," &c., &c.

New York:

CARLTON & LANAHAN,

805, BROADWAY.

1869.

PREFACE.

The accompanying Sermons on "Misread Passages of Scripture" form part of a series which the author projected, but which through ill health he has been unable to complete. He sends them forth in this imperfect form, in compliance with the wish of the publishers; and in the belief too that the topics of some of them will not be without interest, in the conflict of thought on theological subjects which waxes rather than wanes year by year.

The reader will see that much space has not been occupied with critical discussions; nor has the author gone out of his way to correct the English version of the Scriptures. He appreciates fully the value of critical inquiries; but it is wonderful how the sense of leading passages of the Bible gets moulded, apart from, and even in defiance of, critical considerations, by the bias of the various theological schools. Each school makes, if not its own version of the Bible, its own interpretation of the leading passages; and tradition plays an important part in the Protestant as well as in the Roman Church. The text being accepted, each party makes its own version of it, and widely different senses are extracted from the same words. Hence it happens that important passages of Scripture have certain ideas associated with them in the popular mind, which, if they are erroneous, are not to be corrected by a simple announcement, on competent critical authority, of the true rendering of the text.

The author of this little volume believes that there are some very popular but very detrimental misapprehensions, not of the true reading only, but of the true bearing of many important passages; and he offers this slight contribution towards a true understanding of them in the earnest hope that it may stimulate some so to search the Scriptures as to find in them not the confirmation of cherished dogmas, far less stones for the slings of theological war, but the Word of Eternal Life.

J. BALDWIN BROWN.

CLAPHAM,
New Year's Day, 1869.

Misread Passages of Scripture.

I.

THE KINGDOM OF CHRIST.

"My kingdom is not of this world."—John xviii. 36.

Perhaps there is no passage of Scripture more constantly misunderstood than these simple words; and certainly there is no misunderstanding of Scripture which has exercised a more detrimental influence on the life and development of the church. The whole passage contains the very marrow of the doctrine of Christ concerning His kingdom. It is the basis of its constitution. To this, its subjects have rightly looked in all ages for instruction as to its fundamental spirit, principles, and aims. Words more solemn, more pregnant, were never spoken in this world, in this universe, than these. They were spoken at the very crisis of universal destinies. They form the dividing line between the two eternities. From eternity all things had been working towards that hour—the consummation of the incarnation; and to eternity the influence of that hour would go forth, remoulding, regenerating all the worlds. Beyond any words that have ever been spoken, these words are worthy of intense and reverent attention. They are the words with which the Son of God passed on to the cross, that He might pass up to the throne.

The two kings stood there in presence. The representative of the king of this world, who wielded all its force and guided all its movements, the man who had but to nod and the whole civilized world trembled and obeyed; and a King, the elements of whose kingship few could discern, who wielded a strange power and produced a deep impression that He had a right to rule over men, but who wore no signs of royalty and laid no claim to the possession of this world's thrones. Nay, a kingdom had been forced on Him, and He escaped as from a deadly danger from the homage of His subjects, while He spake to them such searching spiritual words that they conceived a great dread of His kingly commands and claims. He bade them begin to rule themselves when they were dreaming of a splendid rule over the gentiles; and He turned inwards on the inner obliquity, foulness, and deformity, those eyes which were watching eagerly for the signs of an approaching advent of a glorious, celestial imperator to the world. Jesus looked on Pilate's kingship, and fathomed it perfectly. He knew from whence the power sprang, and by what springs it was fed, which seated Pilate's master on the world's imperial throne. Pilate found the royalty of Jesus unfathomable; none of his worldly experiences helped him to understand it. Art Thou a king then, poor, worn, tear-stained Outcast, forsaken of every subject, of every friend, in the hour of Thy bitter need? And yet the nascent smile of scorn was checked by something which cast a spell even on that worn-out profligate's heart. That lonely wasted Man there had that about Him which made the representative of the world's master afraid. It seemed mere idle talk to a man like Pilate: "a kingdom not of this world;" "witnessing to truth;" "disciples of the truth:" it was all childish to the trained intellect of this experienced ruler; and yet there seemed to be some power beyond the grasp of his intellect, which something within him recognised, and which might create and rule a kingdom after a fashion which till then had never even crossed his dreams. But to him the mystery remained insoluble. He wrote a title to which his instinct gave a reality that his intellect denied, "Jesus of Nazareth,

KING OF THE JEWS." And here in this passage we have the Lord's own declaration of the constitution and aims of His kingdom; the kingdom which, from that hour, has been the ruling element in the history of this world, and, as we learn from the Apocalypse, of all the worlds of the great universe of God. And men persistently misread it as they misread Him, and employ His words as they employed His works, to frustrate the purpose for which He entered into the world.

Let us see how the misunderstanding of these words arose.

"My kingdom is not of this world:" literally "not from," originally "out of" this world. A clear understanding of the full force of this will give us the clue to the interpretation of our Lord's words. There is an old sense of the preposition "of," which closely corresponds with the full sense of the word employed in the Greek, expressing "out of," "springing from." But "of," like other words and other things, in the course of time has got weakened by the wear and tear of life; and the sense "belonging to," "connected with," is its natural suggestion to modern ears; whereby the sense of our Lord's words has been grievously weakened too. Did the Lord mean to say, "My kingdom has nothing to do with the institutions and arrangements of the worldly life of men: you need not fear any rivalry, delegate of Cæsar; My kingdom is in a quite different sphere, and will keep there, without touching yours: it only has to do with men as spiritual beings, with a view to their final destiny in the eternal state: keep to your secular province, and we shall never cross or clash: the two spheres are quite separate, and nothing but mischief can come of their commerce: I leave you to rule; leave Me to teach, unfettered by conditions; for I aim at no influence on earth, My one object is to persuade men to live a life separate from this world, as much detached as possible from its interests and pursuits, that they may enter into My heavenly kingdom when death releases them, and where the sphere will be all My own"? Was this His meaning? or did He mean to say, "My kingdom is not out of this world; it comes down into this world from on high: this world is, like man, made of the dust of the earth, 'of the earth, earthy,' except some spirit breathe into it from the higher world—then it lives: My kingdom comes to the kingdoms of this world, the interests, aims, pursuits, and common life of men, like this breath of Divine inspiration: without it they all languish and must perish; with it they live: it is a descent of heavenly truth, heavenly love, heavenly life, into the sphere of the earthly, to make it live anew; the earth languishes for My kingdom, for without Me it dies: leave Me free to fulfil My mission, not because this world is nothing to Me, and My kingdom will not trouble itself with its affairs, but because My truth, My life, My love are needful to the life of this world as vital air to the body; because all business, all domestic life, all friendship, all society, all government, all thought, all art, all learning are waiting, are panting, for the living baptism which I bring. I am not of the world, My kingdom is not of the world, in the springs of its influence; it is essentially of heaven, and from heaven: but it seeks the world as the sphere of its influence, the field of its conquest, the realm of its rule. With yearning desire, eagerly as man yearns for fellowship, a friend for the brother of his spirit, the bridegroom for the bride, I seek and claim this world as My own"?

Here are the two ideas of the meaning of these words of our Lord set fairly against each other. The number of those who would deliberately adopt and justify the former is happily growing less year by year. Were we caring only for formal misunderstandings of important passages of Scripture in these discourses, it would be hardly worth while to discuss seriously a perversion which is vanishing with the changed aspects of the times. But the spirit, the savour, of an error continues long to work after it has been formally exploded; and we discuss this passage in this present discourse under the strong conviction that the false view which we have described above continues to tincture very deeply our theology, our preaching, and our social ideas and habits, even in those who would utterly repudiate the formal idea of the Lord's kingdom on which it rests.

Some of the results of this misconception of the true nature of the kingdom have been as follow :—

1. The idea has been widely entertained that the aim of the Lord has been, not to save the world, but to save a chosen few out of the world, leaving calmly the great mass to go to wreck. The favourite notion has been that the Lord's disciples have been in all ages, and still will be, an isolated band, like Israel in Egypt; hating the world around them, hated by it, and waiting only the happy opportunity, the hour of deliverance, to pass out of it triumphant, and leave it to perish by the strokes of the Lord's avenging hand. This idea, that the Church is a little band of chosen ones in the midst of a hostile and reprobate world, is a very favourite one with the disciples in all ages; and it is nourished by the tone in which the apostles wrote and spoke to the few poor men and women who were to begin the work of restoration, and who needed to be upborne against tremendous pressure by the assurance of the special and personal intervention of the God of heaven on behalf of the little company whom He loved. They needed a strong support against a world which was bent on destroying them as it had destroyed their Lord; and so the apostle wrote, "But ye are a chosen generation, a royal priesthood, an holy nation, a peculiar people, that ye should show forth the praises of Him who hath called you out of darkness into His marvellous light. Which in time past were not a people, but are now the people of God; which had not obtained mercy, but now have obtained mercy." "Fear not, little flock; it is your Father's good pleasure to give you the kingdom." That the disciples have been the few in all ages is alas only too palpable to those whose sight pierces

no farther than Elijah's, and who cannot fathom the secret things which are unveiled to the eye of God. But it is a dark heresy to believe that the Lord meant that His own should be the few in all ages, and that the rescue of an election from the impending ruin can satisfy the heart of Him who cried, as the hour of His anguish drew nigh, "And I, if I be lifted up from the earth, will draw all men unto me."

2. Closely associated with this is the notion that all which belongs to the earthly life of men has a certain taint of evil upon it, is corrupt and corrupting in its very nature; so that if a disciple touches it he must touch it like pitch, cautiously, and expect contamination with all his care. That if he must enter into the world's activities, buy, sell, and get gain, marry and give in marriage, rule households and take part in the government of states, he must do it under protest and under the spur of a sharp necessity, and is bound to long anxiously for the time when the need of all this will be over, and he will be free to meditate on Divine things and to praise through eternity. If Christ's kingdom be not of this world, he argues, then all which is of this world, politics, literature, art, society, trade cannot be of Christ's kingdom; and His subjects, hampered by these evil cares for a time, must be ever looking forward eagerly to the day when they will be freed from them for ever. And this is the meaning which is constantly veiled under the phrase, "the coming of the Lord Jesus," and expressed in the prayer, "Even so, Lord Jesus, come quickly."

3. Then further there is the notion that it is only in a very partial sense that we can talk of Christ's kingdom here, that it belongs essentially to the future and eternal state, and can only be fully comprehended by him who can separate it in thought from all the blemishes and accidents of time, and behold it, pure from the defilement and degradation of the earthly (that is the human) in this world, in its glorious Divine form in eternity.

And surely there is a great truth here. The perfect image of it, as Plato said of the polity of which he dreamed, abides only in the heavens; and we need to refresh both courage and hope, when we see the blots and fractures of the kingdom here, by contemplating the pure form of it which abides in the heavens with God. But dreams and contemplations will never bring it down from the heavens; it is here, or nowhere. It is this earthly image which is to be translated into that heavenly likeness; and if we would be near to and like the King, we must follow Him into the very heart of the world's business and throngs, not that we may seek His chosen there and rescue them from the world, but that we may rescue the world from all that makes it other than Christ's kingdom, by driving out of it "everything that defileth, or worketh abomination, or maketh a lie," and thus purify its atmosphere, cleanse the ducts and channels of its life, invigorate its energy, and consecrate its activity, till it grows like its ideal in heaven.

And what has been the history of the kingdom? Since the first hour of its establishment, perpetual intervention in an action upon the worldly affairs of men. It is literally true that Dean Milman's history of Latin Christianity is the completest history of the Western European world during the middle ages, extant in our language. And why? Because during the middle ages, and until now, the Church has been the backbone of human society. All man's dearest interests and hopes have gathered around the kingdom; over its destinies, and under its banners, all man's deadliest battles have been fought. "Yes!" it may be answered; "but this is just the corruption of the kingdom; because it mixed itself with worldly affairs, and suffered worldly men to administer it, it became the centre and pivot of all the movements of human society." But this state of things was at any rate the confession that the men of this world could not get on without the kingdom, that when it was once revealed it inevitably tended to gather around itself all the vital activity of the world. Since Christ appeared, men have felt everywhere that they must place themselves and their concerns in some kind of vital relation to the Church. And this has been the key to the public life of Christendom; in fact it has made Christendom in opposition to heathendom, as the province of all the most cultivated and progressive races of mankind. The forms of relation which men created were no doubt worldly enough; but the sense that they needed the relation, and must find it to live out a true man's life was not worldly, but true, noble, and Divine. The Church from the very hour of the ascension of its Head, began to act on human society as incomparably the most powerful influence extant in the world. It literally re-made society from the very foundations. Far from contenting itself with mastering the will of individual subjects, and wooing them away from the pursuits and interests of the world around them, it entered the homes of men, and cast out the harpy passions which had befouled them; it gave marriage new sacredness, parents new authority and new responsibility, and children new grounds of obedience to their sires. It entered the market and established just weights and balances, honest word, and loyal trust. Theft could be no virtue, and lying no graceful accomplishment, where it established its reign. It entered states, and changed tyrants into kings, serfs into subjects, slaves into freemen, nobles into guardians, pastors, and captains of industry to the poor. That very Rome which doomed the King to a malefactor's death, it entered as a conqueror, and it broke that proud empire to fragments. The time came when Rome could live no longer in the moral atmosphere which it created; and then it summoned purer, nobler, hardier races to occupy the homes and to till the fields which Rome had depopulated and destroyed. It introduced its laws into every code in Christendom. King Alfred begins his statute book by reciting the laws of the kingdom of God.* In truth it has penetrated and permeated every vein and fibre of human society, and it has made it all anew. There is literally nothing with which you in this nineteenth century can concern yourself,—trade, literature, politics, science, art, government, social and domestic life, human rights, human duties, human powers, human fears, aspirations, hopes and joys,—there is not one element of our complex social and political life which is not what it is, because eighteen centuries ago the Lord Jesus witnessed this good confession before Pilate "Thou sayest that which I am, a king." From the world it has asked nothing, taken nothing, but its reverence and love: of the world in that sense it has never been. But in the world, and through the world, the stream of its heavenly virtue and life has wandered, and the wilderness and the solitary place have been made glad by it, and the desert has rejoiced and blossomed as the rose. It has sought studiously to mix itself up with all the relations and interests of mankind; it has a word about them all, it has a law for them all; the weight in the pedlar's bag, the sceptre of the monarch on the throne, are alike under its rule and cognisance, for it claims man as man to be its subject. It says that man was made to be the subject of this kingdom, and all man's life is the true domain of its sway. It looks upon this worldly life of ours—our life as men of this world—as the most solemn, most sacred thing in this universe; God's school of culture of the beings who are to fill His heavenly kingdom through eternity. It cannot spare one relation of men, one art, one industry, one field of activity, one interest, one joy, one hope, one love, from its domain of

* King Alfred's "new book of laws" opens with the sentence, "And the Lord spake all these words and said, I am the Lord thy God," etc. Then follows the decalogue; and then, "Whatsoever ye would that men should do unto you, that do ye also unto them." Besides, there are many passages quoted from the word of God, with most wise reflections on them and applications of them to the matter in hand; and then he proceeds to the laws of the realm.

empire. The whole man, the whole world, in the wholeness of its life, it claims absolutely; and it aims to present the whole man and his whole life, body, soul, and spirit, perfect before the presence of His glory at last. "I beseech you therefore, brethren, by the mercies of God, that ye present your bodies a living sacrifice, holy, acceptable unto God, which is your reasonable service."

And now let me ask your attention to some principles which are suggested by a true understanding of this statement of our Lord.

1. His kingdom is not *of* this world. It is from above, and all the springs of its power are above. The attempt to help it from beneath, to bring the strength, the riches, the honour of this world to help the Spirit who is from above in the work of the kingdom, cripples its energies, frustrates its aims, and exhausts its life. Its one power is the power of truth; "to this end was I born, for this cause came I into the world, that I should bear witness unto the truth," said its Founder and King. It has absolutely no other power. "Every one that is of the truth heareth my voice;" and all the efforts of men to force, tempt, or bribe mankind to support it, but silence that witness, which is all that it asks to win the world to itself.

One can understand the argument of those who support a state establishment of religion and the whole apparatus by which men seek to win for it the supremacy to which it rightfully aspires. They say, "It is of God, it is the heavenly truth, it is worthy of all that men can give to it and of all the power which man can bring to bear on the accomplishment of its work: the state does itself honour, and gives itself stability by supporting it; monarchs are never so royal as in lending to it their influence; all the world's riches are never so precious as when they are poured into its treasuries, and are employed in the promotion of its ends."

And this is no more than the simple truth. The kingdom is worthy to receive the tribute of all the monarchs, the nobles, the wise ones, the rich ones of the world: the more it has of the good-will and help of every man, from the king to the beggar, the better for the kingdom, the better for mankind. All that we say is, Let it win them. Let it win in its own way, by putting forth its own power, the nursing care of the noble, the rich, and the wise. Leave it to employ its own spiritual force to do this and all at which it aims. Lend your heart to it, your hand, your tongue, your pen, your purse, and everything else which it can command and use to win its way to human hearts. But if you bring your human authority to bear to win from your subjects and dependants an outward homage, if you endow it with dead gifts administered by the scribes and lawyers of this world, if you lend worldly pomp and power to those who claim to be its ministers, you oppress and stifle it, and destroy its power of progress in the world. It wants free air, the free air of willing obedience, loyalty, and love. Rob it of that, it dies. It is not of this world. Every gift that is wrung for it from an unwilling hand beggars it. Its riches are the gifts of free will. Mere gold, with no spirit of loving loyalty in the giver, is worse than dross to it; it cankers and eats into its life. The power which has troops of soldiers and legal tribunals behind it blights it by its very breath. All that it asks is freedom; power to do what Christ did, in the way in which He did it; power to bear witness to the truth, and weaken the long silent echoes of truth in human hearts. We have cut off its heavenly connection, and rooted it in the powers and policies of this world; and now we wonder that it languishes, and that one half the people in a Christian kingdom believe nothing of its truth and care nothing for its King. Oh! for the days of apostolic trust and simplicity, when the disciples, "continuing daily with one accord in the temple, and breaking bread from house to house, did eat their meat with gladness and singleness of heart, praising God and having favour with all the people." Oh!

for the baptism of Pentecostal fire from on high. Oh! for one of the days of the Son of Man, whom the Father sent into the world, armed with no authority but that of truth, clothed with no power but that of love. How eagerly then, eager as the thirsty earth when the sound of rain is in the sky, would men drink in the words of Him who had more faith in the power of truth to conquer hearts than in the arms of twelve legions of angels, and whose supreme trust was in the all-mastering force of a love stronger than death—a love that laid down its life that death might not for ever tyrannise over the world.

2. Make your life, your man's life in its wholeness the domain of its empire in you. Beware of a double allegiance. How earnestly and emphatically the Lord denounces it: "Ye cannot serve God and Mammon." Beware of yielding to Christ a part of the empire which is all His own. Beware of that fatal distinction between the man as a Christian, and the man as a citizen, the man as a man of business, which has grown out of the misunderstanding of the principle laid down by our Lord. Christian saint, Christian worshipper, Christian citizen, Christian merchant, Christian parent, be Christian wholly. Refuse to touch a thing in any department of your activity, which will not square with your Christian ideas and aims. Let your daily transactions be as freely open to Christ's inspection as to the world's honourable judgment: let it be the aim of your life at home, abroad, in the shop, the exchange, the forum, to show what the laws of Christ's kingdom can make of a life which is square with their precepts. Adorn the doctrine of God your Saviour, not by fellowship with His people only, but by winning men to worship Him by the spectacle of your diligence, your industry, your purity, your truth, your charity, gentleness, patience, faith, and hope in God; and when they learn that these are the King's gifts to you, at once the signs and the fruits of His reign, they will, like the people of old, break forth into thanksgiving, and confess joyfully that God is with you of a truth.

3. Count it your chief work on earth to be His fellow-helper in His kingdom; help to win for Him the empire of the world.

His kingdom is not of this world. But it is over this world, and it claims this world as its own. The Lord has a heart so large that only the world can fill it. He uttered its whole longing as He entered the cloud of the last agony:—"And I, if I be lifted up from the earth, will draw all men unto me." Bear witness in the world that the one thing needful to it is Christ. Tell statecraft that it needs the laws of the kingdom, to regulate its methods and to indicate its ends. Tell monarchs that they need to observe *the* Monarch, that their rule may be a benediction to loyal subjects instead of a curse to cringing slaves. Tell citizens that they need to become citizens of this kingdom, that the commonwealth on earth may be the image and the vestibule of the commonwealth of the skies. Tell classes that they need the instructions of this Master, that society may be less a den of selfish contentions, and more a field of gracious ministries and ennobling toils. Tell commerce that she needs the inspiration of this duty, that the dull, the common, the base may be transfigured and wear the forms of beauty, nobleness, and truth. Tell life that it needs the quickening of this spirit, that it may not drop piecemeal through the corruptions of sin into the darkness and rottenness of the pit. Above all, tell every soul that hears you, that it needs Christ, the living Bread; the bread of Christ's truth, the bread of Christ's life, the bread of Christ's love, that it may not settle into the darkness of death for ever, but "have everlasting life," where Christ lives and reigns at God's right hand eternally.

II.

THE DUES OF CÆSAR AND OF CHRIST.

"Render therefore unto Cæsar the things which are Cæsar's; and unto God the things that are God's." —MATT. xxii. 21.

WHAT things are Cæsar's? Clearly the things which bear his image and superscription; the things on which he has the right and the power to imprint his mark.

What things are God's? Clearly those things which bear His immediate mark and superscription, which belong to the diviner part in man, which are in man by the breath of the Divine inspiration, and which God claims, and therefore has the right to claim directly and exclusively for Himself. The Lord will not stand between Cæsar and that which bears his image; let not Cæsar dare to stand between God and that in man which bears His image, and which He claims to rule directly by His word and by His Spirit indwelling in human hearts.

This text is constantly quoted to justify the refusal to pay to Cæsar the tax, be it church-rate or anything else, which he may demand for the support of a spiritual system, which we may not believe to be in accordance with the Divine will. I confess that the teaching of our Lord in these words seems to me to point in precisely the opposite direction. The argument which one often hears is to this effect: Cæsar is intruding into God's province when he demands anything from us for spiritual uses; this is a department with which he has nothing whatever to do, and we are giving him that which is God's if we yield to his claims. God alone has the right to claim anything at our hand for spiritual uses; and we are wronging Him, we are robbing the Lord of what political theologians call His "crown rights," if we give unto

Cæsar one farthing for the maintenance of any Church system or systems, or any spiritual operations of any sort, since these are of the things which belong to God alone. The argument of our Lord in these verses points surely the other way. With Him the test of the demand is not the purpose, but the thing demanded. If what is asked has Cæsar's image on it, enough; let him have it; the responsibility of using it rests with him. If Cæsar asks that which has not his image upon it, which he cannot compel before his tribunals or distrain by his officers, such as your judgment, your conscience, and the support of your voice and your hand, obey God rather than man. If you yield to Cæsar, yield because you see that it is right in God's sight, that it is a duty to God to yield to him; if you refuse, refuse because to yield would be wrong in God's sight, and then be prepared to sustain your refusal even unto death.

Do not misunderstand the difficulty of the Jewish rulers, which was a very real one. It was a case of conscience with them. They did not care about the amount of the tribute, that was a small matter; but Cæsar was a Gentile, idolatrous prince. Idolatry was the state religion of the Roman empire. It was a bitter thought to the Jew that an idolater, one capable of setting up his own image in the holy of holies, should rule over him and exact his tribute. Was it not a betrayal of duty to God to consent to it? Was it not right to suffer any extremities rather than yield to the imperial claims? There was a party among the Jews who felt so grievously the degradation and the burden on their consciences, that they were in a chronic state of rebellion against Rome. They were always seeking to foment the differences between their own and the Roman government; and they were prepared to stake their own lives and the life of the nation on their fealty, as they understood fealty, to God alone. It was one of the questions most eagerly debated among them, which they asked the Saviour to solve. A case of conscience,—conscience grieved by being compelled to support a system of government other than that which they believed had been ordained to them of God. Our Lord's solution is most original and striking; and it offers the clearest guidance to us through the multitude of kindred perplexities which cannot fail to arise by reason of the ever varying relations of the secular and spiritual powers in every age of the world. (Matt. xxii. 15–22.) The image on the tribute money settled the matter. This is *primâ facie* evidence that Cæsar has a right to claim it. The power of putting an image on the money marks it as a thing between you and Cæsar. You accept it and use it in daily life, at Cæsar's hand. That image on the penny, the right of coining money being represented by it, is the symbol of all the order and benediction which flow to you from Cæsar's rule; and Cæsar's right to exact it back again is distinctly a question between you and the earthly monarch, into which you have no right to drag, for the purpose of protest, the name of God. Cæsar is ordained of God to take visible charge of this department, the order of civil society; and he and you must settle between you the fair adjustment of his claims. A piece of money bearing Cæsar's image is no battleground for the rights of God. Pay whatever Cæsar asks for his purposes, no matter what they may be, so long as by using Cæsar's mintage you give the stamp of your acquiescence to his rule; and if his purposes seem to you to be wrong, fight him with nobler things than pennies—with voice and pen, the free utterance of opinion, and, if needs must be, in the last extremity, with swords.

If Cæsar asks your homage to his idol, the bending of your knee, or the acclamation of your voice, the answer is clear,—Thy image and superscription are not here; my knee is for my God, my voice is for my God; and all the powers of the universe cannot bend the one or awaken the other without my will. Here I follow the Divine precedent: "Nebuchadnezzar spake," etc. (Dan. iii. 14–18.) But if Cæsar asks my pennies for any purpose which he comprehends within the aim of his government, let him have them; they clearly belong to his sphere. I scorn to hold back what his force can wring from me the next moment; they are his, the responsibility of taking them is his, and the responsibility of using them is his. If I am not satisfied with his use of them, I have nobler means of protest and influence; or, in the last extremity, I can go forth from his empire and have done with him and his pennies for ever.

This is the principle on which it seems to me right to act in church-rate matters. Suppose that one were living in a neighbourhood in which the church of the district had been built under a special act of parliament, to be paid for by a rate levied on the householders during a term of years. It would be our duty to pay year after year our share of the tax which parliament imposed. The money asked for has Cæsar's image and superscription on it: by using it we consent to Cæsar's sway. We have no right to pick and choose which claims of a government we will honour, and which we will refuse. We get the good of the government as a whole, and we pay its claims as a whole, always endeavouring by moral means to secure that the adjustment shall be righteous and fair. And so it may become a clear duty to pay for the building of a church which we never enter, and whose minister regards our ministry as an unauthorized and mischievous intrusion on his sacred domain. If the Church, by Cæsar's ministry, will have our tribute money, we say, Take it; and if the demand be very harsh or peremptory, we say, Take it, in very scorn. But God forbid that we should ever consent to belong to a Church which can condescend to take tribute by force of the unwilling, and which gives the adversary thereby such strong temptation to blaspheme.

Such seems to me to be the bearing of this principle on this and kindred questions. It seems to me distinctly to enjoin on us the course which it is constantly quoted as denouncing. The money Cæsar needs, for the carrying on of his government in the best way he can, is the first charge on the property which the order of civil society suffers us to possess and enjoy. God claims none till Cæsar is satisfied; for Cæsar's claim is His ordinance. Having satisfied Cæsar, take counsel with him about the rest.

But these reflections open up many, some of them perplexing, questions, on which this seems to me a good opportunity to offer some brief remark.

1. Does not Christ in this place seem to recognise some divided allegiance—man under two masters, owing duty to Cæsar, owing duty to God? Will he not be puzzled perpetually to determine their limits, and to settle what is secular and what is sacred? and is there not something repugnant to the very essence of Christianity in the idea that man at any moment, in any relation, can have to do with another being than God? Is not God the sole Lord of his being and of his life? What can be Cæsar's, in contradistinction to that which is God's? I think I have learnt from the Scripture, and I am always preaching the doctrine, that God claims the man in his wholeness; that body, soul, and spirit, riches, knowledge, power, and love, all belong to Him; that there is but one empire, one service, one King; that life is simple, simple as the infinite God. *"Thou shalt love the Lord thy God with all thy heart, and soul, and mind, and strength," "and Him only shalt thou serve." "This do, and thou shalt live."* What claim can Cæsar have on man then, which is not also God's claim? What tribute can one pay to Cæsar, which is not also paid to God? None, absolutely none. The Lord recognises no divided allegiance; His words rightly understood are in perfect harmony with the doctrine of His own sole and supreme lordship over every thought, every passion, and every possession of man. *"Render unto Cæsar the things which are Cæsar's."* Why? Who ordains it? Who has the right to demand it? God. Within the sphere of Cæsar's government, obey him, not because Cæsar can force you, but because God will have you; make it a part of your Divine obedience, to obey wisely and loyally as a subject and a citizen; and

consider that Cæsar claims your service within the sphere which belongs to him, as the ordained minister and representative of God. There is no secular and sacred since Christ appeared. It is all sacred. Civil obedience is an ordinance of the Church. The Scripture bears most explicit witness to these principles wherever it touches on the relations of civil society and its institutions. (1 Pet. ii. 13–17; Rom. xiii. 1–7; 1 Tim. ii. 1–4.) It is God's institution. He sustains it; He, through the ruler, claims your tribute; the result, the order and progress of society, is His work. Innocent III. was right, though in a sense of which he little dreamed. The moon has its own relation to the earth; but they have a common relation to the sun. The moon's orbit is included in the earth's orbit; but the sun sways and balances both of them, and there is not a movement of the moon in obeying the inferior earthly attraction which is not also an act of obedience to the superior sphere. So God has set us under rulers, in societies, as a kind of interior province of His kingdom; but our loyalty as subjects, our duty as citizens, are alike part of the one duty which we owe to God. There is no schism in the body of our service, no double authority in our Lord's realm. The two worlds, the two services, the two spheres, are one in Christ. *"One is your Master, even Christ." "Thou shalt worship Him, and Him only shalt thou serve."*

2. It is needful to inquire how far this principle of obedience is to carry us.

If the money has Cæsar's image and superscription, let him have it; he has a right to it, and in recognising that right we are fulfilling so far our duty to God. Here is a clear and simple principle: but is it a sufficient guidance? does it provide for all the possible exigencies of social and political life? How about the right of resisting Cæsar, when he rules unrighteously? How about John Hampden's refusal of the ship-money, and the grand and glorious struggle which it inaugurated, by which our liberties were won? This is a very grave and important question, and one which, having voluntarily selected such a subject as this, we have no right to pass by. There is a Divine precedent here. (1 Kings xii. 12–24.) What is it which is ordained of God in government? Not any particular king, nor any particular form or institution, but the good of men in the order of civil society. This it is at which God aims, and to this end kings and institutions are His ministers. The king or institution which may best assure this end is the open question in the settlement of which God demands the concert and co-operation of mankind. Every king, every magistrate, every political institution, has a certain Divine sanction, inasmuch as it is the keystone of the arch which He has built, and under whose sheltering dome we live and work. But a keystone which, instead of securing the arch, threatens its stability, has no Divine sanction longer than for the time during which it can be successfully replaced or repaired. The Divine shield is cast, not around the particular king, but around the society and the civilization of which he is the head. It is only in the unity of the society that the Lord's sanction upholds him; let him mar that unity or distract it, and God passes to the side of those who are seeking to set up a new and real keystone in his room. There is nothing like the duty of passive obedience to tyrants implied in the text, or enjoined in the word of God. "*Render unto Cæsar the things which are Cæsar's,*" while Cæsar is the recognised lord. In those crises of history in which Cæsar has to be weighed in the balance, in which the question has to be tried, Who is king and by what rule shall he reign? godly men have to keep clear before the mind's eye what God means by human society, what He aims at, and to help Him, yes, help Him to secure it. If no Cæsar be worth recognising, or Cæsar be altogether too bad to be borne, then refuse his tribute, resist his myrmidons, draw the sword of the Lord and of Gideon to strike for deliverance. The Lord is the Cæsar of such an hour; the Captain of the Lord's host, His sword drawn in His hand as at Jericho, is in these times of revolution busy among men. They best honour Cæsar and serve Christ in such hours, who have the clearest eye for the good of the commonwealth, and who prepare the way for the reign of a Cæsar who, like David, shall rule according to the will of God. The sacred sense of the obligations of a subject or a citizen which those cherish, who have learnt from Christ "by whom kings reign and princes decree judgment," and who know that obedience to the powers that be is a form of obedience to God, makes them patient, beyond the measure of mere political patience, of the weaknesses, follies, and sins of the men who occupy the world's high places; while it makes them stern and firm as death when God has pronounced the sentence of deposition, and has bared the avenging sword and committed it to their hands. These are the men who, like Cromwell, do their work with a terrible force and completeness, and who read lessons in God's name to Cæsars, which remain doctrinal through all time.

3. Surely our Saviour intends us to understand how little money, or anything with Cæsar's image and superscription upon it, can do to make or to mar the fortunes of God's kingdom, which spreads and rules like the dawn, like the moisture in the south wind, like the blush of spring, like the splendour of summer, like everything that is quickened by the breath of God. Tribute! We are always perplexing ourselves about tribute—a steady stream of regular contributions, a flood-tide of golden gifts. It is our measure of power. Quite other is Christ's. His power flashes like lightning from one part under heaven, and shineth to the other part which is under heaven. The world flashes into light, glows into life in a moment, when the times of refreshing, of quickening, come down from God. Men catch it from each other's eyes, each other's lips. It spreads as flame, and gathers strength as it widens its circuit. Money, social and political influence, the force of this world, all that seems solid and potent to men while they are enacting the masque of life which we call living, faint back like rush-

lights in the lightning's flash, like aged institutions in the hour of revolution, when the breath of the Spirit as at Pentecost is falling on the world. I speak, and I am quite sure the sacred writers spoke, in no scorn of money. No *thing* is base: we keep our hate, our scorn, for base spirits, not for things. But for money Paul must have starved, and the kingdom must have perished in its birth. What the Lord means us to understand is that money is the inevitable satellite of higher things. Spirits in earnest movement sweep it with them in their course, as the earth sweeps its atmosphere. Give us hearts of fire, fire that kindles and flashes from heart to heart, from peak to peak of the human; and what work will wait long for gold? Men who in common levels of interest dole out their tens and hundreds, and feel some dull glow of satisfaction stirring the stagnation of their hearts, scatter forth their thousands when God fires their spirits, and their whole being is alive and thrills with joy. Money! nothing greatly spiritual was ever made by money, or was ever marred by money in this world.

There is a touch of scorn in the Saviour's words, "*Shew me the tribute money.*" Scorn of the vain worldly mind that was perplexing itself about tribute, while the love of God and the belief in judgment were fast dying out of human hearts. One sacred conviction in their hearts would have answered the question, and lifted them above the sphere of tribute—as Paul was lifted—into the region of that kingdom which would sweep Cæsar's as a satellite in its sphere. Did the Lord foresee sadly the scene from which a few dark days divided them, when they would yield to Cæsar—these men, who were groaning and haggling over the tribute—absolutely everything that was God's? (John xix. 7–16).

The leader of the band who turned the world upside down witnessed this confession, "*Silver and gold have I none; but such as I have give I thee: in the name of Jesus Christ of Nazareth, rise up and walk.*" They were poor as beggars, but richer in power to draw forth the treasures of this world than kings. What king's command could have wrought this miracle? *"And the multitude of them that believed were of one heart and of one soul: neither said any of them that ought of the things which he possessed was his own; but they had all things common."* (Acts iv. 32.) In truth, this love of Christ is the universal solvent. Nothing remains any man's own when once the heart is touched by this Divine fire. It melts all selfish separations and appropriations, as sun-warmth the bonds of winter, and quickens in the universal human heart the glow and circulation of the spring. Nothing starves in summer for want of the bread that perishes; supplies lie thick everywhere around. And no Divine work stays for lack of the gold that perishes, when once the sun of the Divine love has loosed men's hearts from the winter of their isolation and selfish grasping care. Don't worry about the tribute. *"Trust in the Lord, and do good,"* and things will right themselves at once. Tribute will pour into the treasury, and even the exactors shall become ministers and yield their willing aid. *"Thine officers shall become peace, and thine exactors righteousness." "Kings shall be thy nursing fathers, and queens thy nursing mothers." "Violence shall be no more heard in thy land, wasting nor destruction within thy borders,"* if the King is in thy palaces; if thy heart, soul, and hand are loyally devoted to Christ. I often think, in these days of grand Christian institutions, with their vast fixed incomes and endowments, and all the magnificent apparatus without which it seems to us the Lord's kingdom must perish out of this land and out of the world, of the little company who trudged wearily about the highways of Palestine, seeking their morning meal from the fig-tree by the wayside, and lodging wherever a poor cottager's faith and love gave them shelter for a night, and who,—beggars as to the things which were Cæsar's, but filled as never men were filled before or since with the things which were God's, faith, hope, joy, truth, wisdom, and Divine charity —went forth in this their might and re-made society: the grandest revolution in the history of this universe, accomplished by its beggars and, as the world thought, its fools. And the fact repeats itself in every revolution. Let a man in any age go forth with the fire of God in him; and the force he wields, the mastery he wins, the new life he quickens in a nation, in a world, pours silent contempt on gold. The gold is gathered, as spirit gathers flesh about it and becomes incarnate; so all that belongs to Cæsar's sphere is at the commandment of that which comes straight from God's and glows with the inspiration of His life. Gifts of a splendid lavishness in such seasons are abundant; and strangely enough the givers feel enriched unspeakably by the joy of giving, enlarged immeasurably by impoverishment, and increased by abnegation. The richest in such seasons are those who give most, not those who have most. A wonderful sense of the glorious wealth of a heart which has a guest-chamber for Christ, and whose pulses beat joyously as the free tide of the Divine love flows through and over it on all around, kindles men's souls to a new conception of riches. It fills the beatitudes with a wonderful meaning, and shows the sorrows and straits of poverty overflowed by the riches and joys of God.

III.

"UNTO THIS LAST."

"I will give unto this last, even as unto thee."—MATT. xx. 14.

THESE words appear at first sight to set us very decisively face to face with the sovereignty of God, in its sternest and most naked form—affirming its right to distribute its gifts and payments at its pleasure, and refusing to consider the question of equity when urged by the creature's sharp complaint. "Take that thine is, and go thy way." "Is it not lawful for me to do what I will with mine own?" "I will give unto this last, even as unto thee." There, it is said, and with apparent truth, is Sovereignty—pure, naked Sovereignty. The "I will" of God seems to be the sole explanation which is vouchsafed of His dispensations and decrees. But this view of the matter has always seemed to me deeply unsatisfactory. Equity is a strong instinctive principle, which God Himself has established in the judgment seat of the human conscience; and God never beats down with the bare assertion of an irresistible Sovereignty the soul that is perplexed about the equity of His ways. It is equity, pure, celestial equity, which reveals itself to those who will search for it in this parable; equity to the poor souls who had been standing all the day idle in the market-place, because no man had called them to the vineyard; equity to the labourers who had borne the burden and heat of the day, and had made the dignity and culture of the Lord's husbandmen their own. It is an equity which invites the closest criticism from those who will search it thoroughly, and which reveals to the searchers deep vital truths about man and about God.

"I will give unto this last, even as unto thee." It is a startling sentence. This man had been labouring in the vineyard under the burning heat, through the blazing noon; he had borne and bent under the whole burden of the work: while this one had been brought in at the eleventh hour, in the cool evenfall, and by a few minutes of light sweet labour he had won the equivalent prize. There is something startling here, and men have felt it; and they have striven in manifold and curious ways to square the method of the Master with their fundamental notions of the righteousness of God. There are theologians who feel no need to square it. According to a theology which has exercised a wide-spread and malign influence in the past, Sovereignty answers amply every difficulty, and treats our ideas of equity as a high impertinence, when they claim to weigh the ways of God. If it pleases God to make some men to be saved and other men to be damned, who shall question His rights? and if He is glorified equally by the salvation of the chosen and the damnation of the reprobate, who dares complain, or to what court can we carry the appeal? There are theologians who would have us rest calmly on the conviction that a sovereign and inscrutable will is ruling, and trouble ourselves in no wise about the equity of the decrees. But one cannot but reflect that this composed contentment with the doctrine of reprobation is mainly conspicuous in those who feel themselves safe from its trenchant stroke. With the exception of Lord Byron—to whose malign and scornful tone we believe that this was the real key—we hardly discover the disciples of the doctrine among those who believe that they are reprobate; and in the case of the theological school whose influence is happily dying away, but which survives in out-of-the-way places to an extent little dreamed of still, we may fairly entertain the question, whether, if it were flashed suddenly on their souls that they, the theologians, were doomed by the Divine decree to everlasting anguish, their rest in the inscrutable Sovereignty would be so calm, and their contentment so assured. For thinkers of this school, of course, such a parable as this presents no sort of difficulty. A penny more or less would not be likely to stagger them, when the gift of heaven or the doom of hell raise no question as to the equity of the Divine decrees. But with the great multitude of Christian thinkers the parable has been the source of much grievous perplexity, as the manifold explanations amply prove. The question is, in which verse of the parable are we to find the key to it? "Unto this last will I give, even as unto thee," states the problem. Is the solution to be found in the body of the parable, or must we seek it outside in a general study of the ways of God?

There can be no question, I think, that the broad bearing of the parable is on the impending revolution in the visible Divine kingdom, whereby, as the Saviour says, the kingdom of God was to be taken from the Pharisees, and "given to a people bringing forth the fruits thereof." I say advisedly, from the Pharisees; from the party which held the chief influence and authority in the Church. Their influence, their standing-ground, was utterly shattered by the Saviour's advent; the kingdom passed visibly, absolutely, finally, out of the rule of their hand. But there was never any question of its passing wholly from the Jews; the Jews were never to be disowned. Paul earnestly, with intense emphasis, asserts this, and makes it the basis of a long and profound argument. "I say then, hath God cast away His people? God forbid. For I also am an Israelite, of the seed of Abraham, of the tribe of Benjamin. God hath not cast away His people, which He foreknew." (Rom. xi. 1, 2.) The Jews, as such, were not cast away. We think all too slightly of the strength of the Jewish element in the apostolic Church. And it is the Jews—the people, not their leaders—who are in question here. They had borne the burden and heat of the day; they had done the work—with what result, well or ill, is not the point in debate. There is no idea of their being dismissed without honour or recompense; the question is simply concerning the bringing in of other husbandmen, the Gentile nations, at the last hour, to share in full measure in all that the Jewish workmen had won by their long and hot day's toil.

Perhaps the favourite mode of reconciling the Master's dealings with fundamental principles of equity is to be found in the suggestion, towards which some sentences in Olshausen's Exposition strongly lean, that the first called laboured so lazily, and the last called so strenuously that (regarding the actual amount of work accomplished) the Master's arrangements were more equitable than might at first appear. Notwithstanding the apt illustration of this which appears to be offered by the history of St. Paul, who, though the last called, "laboured more abundantly than they all," the explanation seems to me to miss the whole point of the teaching of the parable, and to proceed upon very low and worldly conceptions of the method of the Divine ways. There is no hint of such a solution in the body of the parable itself; which is a sufficiently grave objection. If this be the key, its existence is carefully suppressed, and the souls that were most sorely perplexed by the appearance of injustice are left wholly ignorant of the truth. Nay, their ignorance is confirmed by the language, or rather by the silence, of the parable. The answer to their protest on the ground that they had "borne the burden and heat of the day" would have been decisive and was ready at hand. But no hint of a justification on this ground is suffered to appear. Their assertion is allowed to pass unanswered, and must be accepted for the purposes of the parable as the truth. Whether they had wrought well or ill, though it may be the main point in other parables, is plainly not the point which is in question here. And in the interpretation of parables we get into endless difficulties, if we, so to speak, travel beyond the record, and consider the details in any other light than as the garniture of the one central idea which the parable is intended to set forth. As far as this parable is concerned, we must accept it as a fact that they had borne the burden and heat of the day; and no explanation of its equity can be entertained which sets that fact at nought.

That we may the better understand what it does mean, let us consider:—

I. The work of the vineyard to which all were called, and in which the first called bore the burden and heat of the day.

II. The reason of the idleness of the husbandmen who at the eleventh hour were called to the work.

III. The Lord's justification of His ways.

I. The work of the vineyard.

I believe that there is nothing very definite in detail here set before our minds, and that we shall get into dire confusion if we inquire about the class or classes of members of the Church which may be signified by the husbandmen. There is no question of classes of Christian labourers, or kinds of Christian work, in the narrative. It is God's work, and these are God's workmen in the field of His visible Church, in the broadest sense which those words may bear. The vineyard is the visible field of God's tillage. The vast invisible field we are not called to consider; except to assure ourselves that one grand principle rules, explains, and justifies God's methods with the whole. The visible field, up to the day of Pentecost, was the Jewish commonwealth, which was about to expand into the Christian commonwealth when our Lord delivered the discourses which contain our text. In the Jewish commonwealth, not priest and prophet only, but every child of Abraham was a called husbandman; just as every Christian disciple, as much as apostle, bishop, evangelist, or deacon, is a called labourer in the wider vineyard of the Christian Church. The broad feature of the work of the vineyard is, that it is man's true, noble, God-ordained work.

It is the work for which all his organs and powers were fashioned, and in which his whole being was made to rejoice. Why were these men standing in the market-place? What took them there? Why were they not lounging idly about the fields, or sleeping at home? Clearly because some divine instinct within them moved them thither, that they might be in the way of being hired for a day's toil. A divine instinct, I say. He little understands humanity, who imagines that the great bread and cheese question is at the bottom of even a tithe of the daily labour of mankind. It would be hard to find a man who just works enough to provide the bread and cheese and beer which he needs to sustain his animal nature, and then folds his arms and takes his ease until new hunger compels new toil. There are such men about the world, no doubt; but it is a hard matter to find them. And when they are found, men attach to such a bestial idea of life the epithet "unmanly" with a bitter emphasis, which reveals how deeply there is inwrought into the very texture of man's nature the divine instinct of work. Man is made for it, as the flower of the field is made for the free air of heaven. Shut out from it, he grows irritable and sickly, his powers droop, his courage fails, his hope dies, his life is a wreck. And very noble motive inspires well-nigh the whole of human labour. Love, pure self-denying love, love of wife, love of child, of friends, of mankind, is the moving spring of most of man's most strenuous toil. God's work, work for God, and for man for the love of God, is but the highest form or mode of human labour. Man's divine work is not something essentially different in principle from all his other work. All his best labour in his daily tasks proceeds upon the existence within him of powers and organs which can only find their highest exercise, and which can only justify their lowest exercise, in the work of the vineyard which the Lord has given us each one to do. Man is simply unmanned while he stands all the day idle in the market-place; his goodliest powers and organs are rusting, his blood trickles with dull stagnant motion through his lazy veins, his whole system is oppressed and burdened, his muscles ache for exercise, his cheek is pale, his eye is dim.

The kingly being is unbraced and discrowned; no joys or honours attend the *fainéant* king.

Who are the pitiable ones here? On whom shall we spend our regrets and sorrows? The hardy sunburnt workmen, who have spent their strength manfully in a brave day's work; who watch the westering sun as only the tired labourer has the right to watch him; and who settle peacefully to the workman's rest till the gay sunlight wakes them again to new glad toils in a young, fresh, dewy world? Nay, the work of the vineyard is man's honour, joy, glory, and bliss. To be called to work in it is the crown of his manhood; to finish his work with joy is his noblest praise. But why should it not end here? If he is to be counted blessed who works in the vineyard, if his work gladdens, enriches, and ennobles him what room is there for the thought of pay? What can the pennies in this case mean?

Man is made with a large capacity, and a large thought and hope of happiness. He can take a large blessing into his being, larger than he can meet within his present sphere. The range of his nature takes in the infinite and the eternal. The work is noble, glorious exercise; but God only can fill and satisfy his spirit. Man needs something beyond the mere play of his powers, though their free play is an intense exhilaration and delight. He needs the fellowship of beings to satisfy the yearning, to feed the appetite, of his nobler nature; he needs the love of God, and communion with all that is of God, that he may rest and be blessed. This is the reward which the earthly day of his toil and patience will bring. The true workman is happy in his work, and sings while he toils. But God has a yet richer benediction for His children when the work is done, a blessing which will beautify and glorify life through eternity. This He gives to the workman out of His royal bounty, His own blessedness. It is His own to give; and all true workmen, whatever the measure of their work, because of the spirit of their work, shall claim it at His hand.

II. The reason of the idleness of the husbandmen who were not called till the eleventh hour to the work.

"And about the eleventh hour he went out, and found others standing idle, and said unto them, Why stand ye here all the day idle? They say unto him, Because no man hath hired us." The true key to the parable lies here. There are many other answers conceivable. They might have said, Because we like to lounge and loaf, work is irksome; or, Because we are over-tired with yesterday's toil; or, Because the pay does not suit us, we are out on strike. Imagine that any one of these answers had been given; the whole character of the parable would have been changed, and the equity of the ways of God would then have been dark, dark indeed. But no. The men were willing to work; they were waiting to be hired; they made no bargain about their pay. "Go ye into the vineyard; and whatsoever is right, that shall ye receive," the Master said; and they went, content to leave their wage to His justice. The men evidently cared more about the work than the pay. In truth the idlers were to be pitied. The Master pitied them, and He gave to their will the wage which lack of opportunity had forbidden them to earn before.

And this opens up some serious thoughts about the pagan world, and its relation to the kingdom of God. There is a profound, but not an impenetrable mystery hidden in the words, "the fulness of the time." Through long ages the pagan world was left groping in the darkness, "*feeling after God if haply it might find Him,*" and moaning as it grasped at phantoms in the gloom, and saw them slip from its empty hand. Looking at the anguish and misery of the world at this moment, one is constrained to confess that the Lord of the world is One who can bring Himself to look upon, and to bear the responsibility of ruling over, a terrible amount of pain. But what shall we say of the long ages of pagan darkness, when men were not *feeling* after God only, but crying for Him, shrieking to Him, were maiming their quivering flesh and torturing their shuddering hearts, because the void only echoed back their own voices and none could tell them the Divine Name. The time is gone by when it was possible to look upon the history of heathendom as the history of one long stern effort to break away from God, to blot out His name from the universe, and to tear every trace of His image out of the life of the human world. It is now well understood that the deepest thing in heathen life and heathen literature was ever the cry after the living God, and the effort to find Him; the grandest passages in the religious records of heathendom are the words in which the founders of the great pagan systems proclaimed what they believed had been made known to them of His Being and His Will; and the gladdest, in truth the only joyous, passages in pagan history, are the records of the generations in which men persuaded themselves that God had at length visited His world. Soon the gladness vanished, overborne by wrong and lust. But while it lasted it made the solitary gleam of brightness which crosses the blackness of the pagan night. The revival of morals, of manners, and of hopes, which for a few brief generations has followed the teaching of the great masters whom paganism adores, is the one ray of heavenly light which shines in the pagan darkness, and bears witness that there is sunlight, though shining on other spheres. The joy which filled the hearts of the heathen peoples, when Sákya-Mouni, Zerdusht, Confucius, or Mahomet, proclaimed at any rate a purer faith, a nobler idea of life, than the dark, soulless, senseless formulæ in which a tyrannous priesthood had buried the Divine Name, is like some faint and far-off glow of the joy which leaped from heart to heart like flame when it was known that God had in very truth visited His people, and that the King of Glory had taken possession of His earthly throne.

Through this long sad night, lit only by these rare faint gleams, men had been looking, longing, and moaning for a deliverer; and steadily settling the while, and they knew it, into the slough of the devil's accursed dominion, because no Almighty Helper and Saviour appeared. We see their misery, their tears, their mad outbursts of passion, their foul orgies of lust; and our hearts bleed, nay there have been hearts that have burst, as they watched this tragedy of despair. And heaven heard it all, saw it all, through long ages; and still no deliverer was sent. It is a profound mystery, the millenniums through which the world was left to grope and to moan in the darkness, while the clear sunlight of God's truth was flashing its brightness so joyously on the homes of the chosen race. I say again, the mystery, though profound, is not inscrutable; for there is Calvary to expound it. In the long run, in the great day of eternity, it will be seen, that this forsaking of the heathen world was an essential part of a benign and merciful plan, of which Calvary is the centre; and that it lies in the full harmony of a love which *"endured the cross, and despised the shame,"* that a whole world might be gathered at length to the great Father's heart. But the *"no man hath hired us"* has a profound and pathetic meaning, when we search the records of pagan religious effort and aspiration, and when we see how everywhere, when the gates were flung open, the Gentiles thronged, streamed, crushed, into the kingdom of God. I find in this thought the whole mystery of the parable unfolded. The Gentiles had been looking, waiting, longing, in their own dull way, for the work of the vineyard. It was the Master's counsel, as well as their own dull hearts, which had kept them idle during the noontide heats. And it was the work which it was in their hearts to do that the Master honoured, when He made them equal to the favoured and happy husbandmen, had they but known it, who had *"borne the burden and heat of the day."*

III. The Master's justification of His ways.

"So when even was come, the lord of the vineyard saith unto his steward, Call the labourers, and give them their hire, beginning from the last unto the first. And when they came that were hired about the eleventh hour, they received every man a penny. But when the first came, they supposed that they should have received more; and they likewise received every man a penny. And when they had received it they murmured against the goodman of the house, saying, These last have wrought but one hour, and thou hast made them equal unto us, which have borne the burden and heat of the day. But he answered one of them, and said, Friend, I do thee no wrong; didst not thou agree with me for a penny? Take that thine is, and go thy way: I will give unto this last, even as unto thee. Is it not lawful for me to do what I will with mine own? Is thine eye evil, because I am good? So the last shall be first, and the first last: for many be called, but few chosen" (Matt. xx. 8—16).

These words imply—

1. That there is infinite grace, through which a certain equity shines, in the things which God has provided for all who have wrought, even though feebly and tardily, at His work. The work is honour and happiness; the want of it is shame and pain. The early labourers are the enviable; the late labourers are the pitiable. But God in His boundless grace adds a boundless gift to all: "the gift of God," which "is eternal life, through Jesus Christ our Lord." But through the grace a certain equity shines. Man was made for Life, he was born for it. To miss the glorious boon which God has the power to bestow on him through Christ, were to miss the very end and issue to which God touched his spirit. A well-nigh infinite capacity of being, loving, and enjoying, is in him, which God only can satisfy and eternity only can complete. And God in His boundless love and mercy meets him in his idleness and degradation, and proposes to him a work which His grace will crown with glorious, everlasting joy.

2. None shall miss the blessing through the order of the dispensations.

If the Jews were called, and the Pagans were left sad

and idle in the streets, the evenfall shall adjust the balance, the evening of earth's life, the morning of the everlasting day. Idle and sad, I say. When you are next at South Kensington Museum, place yourself before the cartoon of "Paul preaching at Athens." Mark the foremost in the group of pagan hearers; he bears in his sad wistful countenance the whole tale of Gentile waiting, longing, hoping, disappointment, despondency, and despair. Few preachers can preach such a sermon as utters itself mutely from that man's eyes and lips. This parable is Christ's answer to the mute appeal: "No man hath hired thee, poor outcast! the day spent, the soul lost! Come in, at the last hour, come in. These have wrought in a noble service the long day through. The sweat of manly toil is on their brow, the joy of a work well done is in their hearts. Come in; the sun still lacks some hours of setting. Bend thy soul to the task, put thy heart into the labour of the hour, and the same meed shall be thine. Even as unto this first, will I give unto thee; come in."

9. On a wider scale the parable is Christ's assurance, that through all outward inequalities of gift, endowment, opportunity, position, prospect, which jar this jangled world, there is a sublime equity ruling which will right all wrongs, adjust all balances, and square all issues with pure celestial justice at last. "*No man hath hired us.*" How much does this explain of the bitterness and misery with which the world is filled! Cross purposes, cross callings, cross relationships, cross necessities, cross issues of life! Men with power in them for a service which is never asked of them; tied down to a desk or a counter, it may be, while they feel within them the stirrings of a power to guide the coursers of the sun. Men bound in a home which has no beauty for them, no love; while beyond there is a vision of the Eden which might be, if bonds could be unbound and bound afresh. Some overflowing with fatherly or motherly tenderness, in a barren home. Some shrinking from the prattle of infant

voices, yet with stuff in them of noble texture, shut up to a nursery through the prime of their days. Some longing, pining, panting for a work they love, bound to a work they loathe. Some with a genial, generous, royal nature, wrestling with the serpents of care and penury their long life through. "This is a mad world, my masters;" "the times are out of joint;" it is all out of joint everywhen and everywhere! "No man hath hired us" to the work which we are fit for; a glorious wealth of being, of power, is left to "fust in us unused."

Patience, brothers, patience! One grand work, the grandest, spreads broad and fair before you; "in your patience possess ye your souls." The hiring is in higher, wiser hands; the patience, the hope, are in yours, with all their glorious eternal fruit. None of the sighing, none of the groaning, none of the desire and yearning of your spirit, is hidden from Him who made you, and who in His own good time will call you to your God-ordained work. "UNTO THIS LAST WILL I GIVE, EVEN AS UNTO THEE" reveals the sublime equity of His dealings. Await with strong patience, with steadfast hope, the things and the times of His sovereign appointment; till you find with profound and wondering joy, that your patience has won a prize whose splendour outshines the constellations, and whose bliss shall outlast eternity.

IV.

LAW AND LIFE.

"In the place where the tree falleth, there it shall be."—ECCLES. xi. 3.

THERE are few passages in the word of God which are more constantly misapplied than this. It is systematically wrested to the establishment of doctrines with which it has nothing whatever to do. The popular interpretation of the text treats it as equivalent to the assertion, that the condition of the human soul through its long eternity is settled absolutely and irrevocably by death. We believe that nine out of ten, of those who hold this doctrine would quote this passage if they were suddenly asked to sustain their belief out of the word of God. With the truth of the doctrine in question we are not dealing in the present discourse; there are passages in the word of God which bear on it with most unquestionable cogency. But this is not one of them. Our present purpose is to show what it *does* mean, and that its reference is to a subject which is well-nigh as far removed from that on which it is supposed to bear as the poles.

We approach a dread, an awful subject, when we contemplate the condition of those who pass into the unseen world impenitent and faithless; who despise finally, as far as we can trace, the riches of the mercy and the love of God. It is a subject which is occupying the most earnest and solemn thoughts of some of the wisest of our Christian thinkers, and on which a large freedom of judgment will have to be conceded within the visible pale of the Christian Church. It is easy to state the doctrine of universalism, and to offer it as a solution of the dark difficulties with which the subject is surrounded.

But it is not easy to get the doctrine of universalism out of the Bible; nay, it is not possible, without grievous violence to some of its plainest and most awful statements: nor, on the other hand, is it easy to harmonize it with any intelligent conceptions of the moral freedom and responsibility of every child of the human race. Others seek refuge, for it is as a refuge that they appear to cling to it, in the theory of annihilation—that is, the annihilation on a vast scale of that which God made to be His masterpiece, which He constituted in His own image, and into which He infused by inspiration the breath of His own life. More grievous violence must be done to the plain language of Scripture by the advocates of this theory than by those of the former; and it seems to us still harder to find for it a place in any intelligent and harmonious conception of the scheme on which God made the worlds.

Were it possible for us to hold it, it would seem to unfold a terrible vision of the issue of the great experiment of creation. The free beings whom God made to be the glory of His universe, drooping down in throngs, after a life struggle full of anguish and despair, into the darkness of the everlasting night! One would be tempted to ask passionately in that case, Why was not the dire experiment of liberty ended in the hour of the first transgression? why was not the free universe, parent of such wrongs and miseries, strangled in its birth?

Nor may we dare to hide from ourselves and others, in these days, the dread considerations involved in the doctrine which the Church has drawn from explicit statements in the word of God. Eternal punishment; eternal suffering in the universe; moans rising up ever in the ear of heaven; the cries of souls in anguish piercing the serenity of the heavenly rest. Eternal evil too. Evil never more to die out of the worlds on which the dew of the primal benediction lay, and which flashed back the smile of Him who looked upon them and saw that "*they were very good.*" The curse rioting, sin reigning unto death, in some region of the universe sustained and ruled by the Divine hand; never to be expelled from the creation, never to be drawn under the merciful reign of God. We are too prone to hide the awful reality which is behind this language, by vague notions of the judgment as the final banishing of evil from the sight of God and of the blessed. Nothing that is can be banished from the sight of God; nothing that exists—we will not say lives, life is a sacred word—can exist from moment to moment without the interposition of the Divine hand. Ever present before the great Father must be the anguish and the moans of the souls in torment; ever to His eye there must be this dark counterfoil to the joy and glory of the redeemed. And yet the question forces itself upon us: What else can the plain statements of the Scriptures mean; nay, what else can in the essential nature of things befal a free spirit that chooses to exercise its freedom in sin? We may well feel with a wise one of old, "Such knowledge is too wonderful for us: it is as high as heaven, what can we do? it is as deep as hell, what can we know?"

Sore difficulties beset us in working out a clear and harmonious theory of the judgment and its issues. But blessed be God that we can rest in the belief that all will be, in ways that we see not, so wisely and righteously ordered by the Judge of all the earth, as to satisfy the yearning heart, not of the great Father only, but of the Redeemer of humanity, and to fill the universe with praise. Here as elsewhere, when we are bewildered and perplexed by thoughts too high for us and which reach too far, we find a sure refuge and rest in faith. We believe God in Christ, and we can leave our future and the future of humanity in His hand. Meanwhile, our work, our duty is clear: "*Now then we are ambassadors for Christ, as though God did beseech you by us: we pray you in Christ's stead, be ye reconciled to God.*" "*This is the work of God, that ye believe on him whom he hath sent.*" "*Other foundation can no man lay than that is laid, which is Jesus*

Christ." "*Believe on the Lord Jesus Christ, and thou shalt be saved.*"

But this is beside the scope of the present discourse. I have to consider what these words, so strangely misapplied, do mean, and to draw from them those most pregnant lessons concerning the conduct of life which they are intended to afford. "*Cast thy bread upon the waters: for thou shalt find it after many days. Give a portion to seven, and also to eight; for thou knowest not what evil shall be upon the earth. If the clouds be full of rain, they empty themselves upon the earth: and if the tree fall toward the south, or toward the north, in the place where the tree falleth, there it shall be. He that observeth the wind shall not sow; and he that regardeth the clouds shall not reap. As thou knowest not what is the way of the spirit, nor how the bones do grow in the womb of her that is with child: even so thou knowest not the works of God who maketh all. In the morning sow thy seed, and in the evening withhold not thine hand: for thou knowest not whether shall prosper, either this or that, or whether they both shall be alike good.*"

I. The key to the passage, the broad idea which underlies the whole, is in the first verse. In the sixth verse the writer repeats the thought under a varied form, and it is evident that it rules the whole. Let us ask ourselves what it means. It is a fair question whether we have here a reference to a popular proverb descriptive of the most useless and apparently hopeless work, "casting bread upon the waters;" or whether there is a reference to Egyptian husbandry, which might seem just as futile a method, did not experience prove that a harvest of spendid abundance is the well-nigh certain result. I do not think that it is needful to settle the rival claims of the two interpretations,* inasmuch as the essential point of the author's meaning is involved in both. In either case

* Those who wish to settle the critical question will find ample help in Dr. Ginsburg's learned and exhaustive "Commentary on Ecclesiastes." (Longmans, 1861.)

you have a husbandry of faith; and in either case you have a grand image of all noble spiritual work. All husbandry is of faith to an extent which we little realize, but most especially this husbandry. The seed-corn scattered from the hand vanishes from sight, the very bed in which it is hidden lies buried, and an uncongenial, impenetrable element spreads its barrier between the sower and the seed, which he must leave in the hands of God. The farmer who has ploughed his field and settled his seed in the furrows feels less shut out from it; he sees at least where it lies, he can test its condition, he can trace the first green bloom on the brown surface of his fields, which is the prophecy and the pledge of harvest. But seed cast into the waters! where is it? who can trace it? what can withhold the waters from rotting it, and burying the promise of the seed and the hope of the husbandman in their depths? And the seed dropped into the furrows of the human seed-field, the heart that has been broken up by the deep ploughshare of God's discipline, and over which a fertilizing flood of quickening influences has passed,—where lies it? What glance can follow it? What hand can touch it? What eye can foresee, what brain can forecast, its destiny? There is a dread likeness here, to the eye of the understanding, between this perilous husbandry and spiritual labour; man's knowledge is so limited, man's hand is so powerless, the seed passes so far out of his ken, and lies buried in such deep depths within.

There is a mystery in all husbandry which it is manifestly the purpose of God to keep clearly before the eye of the soul. He will not suffer us to forget it. "*And he said, So is the kingdom of God, as if a man should cast seed into the ground; and should sleep, and rise night and day, and the seed should spring and grow up, he knoweth not how. For the earth bringeth forth fruit of herself; first the blade, then the ear, after that the full corn in the ear. But when the fruit is brought forth, immediately he putteth in the sickle, because the harvest is come*" (Mark

iv. 26–29). This is the daily miracle of nature, the "sign" which is done daily before our eyes. There are those, and they constitute a large and powerful school of thinkers in our day, who refuse coldly to listen to any evidence as to the miracles of Scripture, and who see this sign of an unseen energy at work around them and within them each moment, but feel powerless even to inquire from what fountain it springs. It is deeply unjust to brand the Positivist school of philosophy as explicitly either materialistic or atheistic. They are by no means blind to the fact that there is a hidden mystery in nature; they see quite as clearly as we do its marvellous depths. There is something quite as wonderful in their sight in the daily growth of the corn and the assimilation of our daily bread, as in the feeding of five thousand in the lonely wilderness by the word which came forth from the mouth of the Saviour. But they say, this region is simply impenetrable by the human intellect; in all its efforts at discovery it simply meets with shadows projected under various conditions and at various angles by itself. Our fair charge against them is, not that they are blind to the fact of a mystery in nature, but that they dishonour the royal faculty of the reason with which God has gifted them, by distrusting its ability to deal with a vast class of phenomena—the manifestations of the working of unseen powers with which God has surrounded them—which are as definite and substantial as the physical facts out of which they educe their laws. The world of spiritual experience and activity with which mainly the Bible deals, claims from us, at any rate, observation, thought, and deduction, as reverent as that which we joyfully devote to the phenomena of nature; and we accept as eagerly the thoughts and suggestions of seers who have insight into this world of mystery, as we accept the teachings of science concerning things which are beyond our sight. And if words come to us from this higher sphere, which harmonize discordant elements and make the chaos of our spiritual consciousness and experience a cosmos ruled by intelligence and love, we joyfully accept the truth which sustains and explains the phenomena, and feel that in proclaiming it we are "holding forth a word of life" to our fellow-men. And the Scripture miracle is to us a flash of sunlight, which illumines the darkness of the unknown: we see unveiled the Hand which is working each moment these signs and wonders within and around us; and, studying the nature, the mind, the heart, by which that Hand is guided, we find rest in the assurance that the power whose awful manifestation in nature might well appal and overwhelm us, is under the absolute rule of One whose declaration of Himself is that He is Love. We receive an emancipation from both the terrors and the idols of the imagination, when we learn that the daily bread of our lives comes to us from the hand of the Father, and is crowned with His benediction. The poor believe it quite simply: they have a beautiful sense of dependence on the Hand which feeds the birds and clothes the lilies. As a child hangs on the mother's breast, they hang daily as trustfully on the bounty of the Lord. And they are more free from vain fancies herein than the philosophers. It is the wise and the scribe who are in bondage to idols: simple hearts, which have received the revelation of the relations of the two worlds which the Bible offers, walk free in the sunlight, and dwell quiet from the fear of evil.

"Cast thy bread upon the waters: for thou shalt find it after many days."

The main point here then is, that in all husbandry there are two elements—the intelligence and energy of the man, and the co-operation of a secret force, the springs of which and the methods of which escape him, but on which absolutely depend all his fruits. Neither without the other can produce the harvest. Paul plants, Apollos waters; but God giveth the increase: but neither without Paul's planting does the harvest spring. *"Behold, a sower went forth to sow."* The human sower is, as far as we see, the indispensable fellow-worker with the

Most High God. But God, and not the human sower, has the absolute control of the result.

Let us look at this more closely. To impress this upon us is the main object of the writer in the text.

II. The writer of this book asks us to consider how much that has the most important bearing on the results of our activity is hopelessly beyond the control of our hand.

No doubt this is a truism: but it is the meaning and force of these truisms which most easily escape us; custom is the blind of truth. No matter what it may be to which we put our hands, we are dealing with elements which only partially subject themselves to our control, or rather reveal to us the secret by which they may be bent to our use. Always there is a large variable element in the problem of our activities; and on this variable element, which we have no means of calculating, depends all that is most precious and vital in our results. Husbandry here is the great witness for, and key to, higher things. Certain bases are fixed and unalterable; else our work would be a pure lottery. Much on which its fruits depend is variable; else our work would be purely mechanical. God gives us a large measure of assurance, that we may work bravely and put our hearts into our labour, as those who have a right to hope that they will carry the sheaves of their harvest home; but He crosses our toil with a zone of uncertainties, that we may be faithful workmen, trusting and praying as well as working, and may be kept in holy and blessed dependence on Him who can lift us above all servile care for immediate results. Consider—

1. The awful force and inevitable certainty of the processes of Nature, the unfailing "order of Nature" which furnishes forth the field of our toils. That order God guarantees. The assurance is thus expressed: "*While the earth remaineth, seedtime and harvest, and cold and heat, and summer and winter, and day and night shall not cease*" (Gen. viii. 22). That word of promise which has

nursed the trembling hope of man into strong certainty—for he is as sure that the sun will rise on the morrow as he is of his own existence—lies at the foundation of all his steady activity as a workman in this lower world. The joyful outgoings of the morning and evening, and the succession of the seasons, are given to him as the constant elements in his husbandry. These are assured to him by the voice that called them into being and the hand which sustains their motions. God tells him that he may count absolutely on this order. And what guarantee, when we come to think of it, have we of that order, but such as a firm belief in an intelligent Ruler of the universe, who sympathises with the hopes and blesses the toils of His children, affords? Then further,—

2. There is the absolutely certain sequence of physical causes and effects, or antecedents and consequents, which we call laws of nature, which vary not one hair's breadth from their ordained order in obedience to the mandates of our will, but which, by observing and mastering the principle of that order, we can use for the accomplishment of our ends. These are our tools to work with. A thousand subtle laws are concerned in every process of the husbandman's toils. On a large scale and in the long run the question of his success depends absolutely on his comprehension and observance of those laws. The progress of man's knowledge of nature is really a progress in the mastery of the variable element in the problem of his labour. A thousand accidents, which baffle the ignorant and careless husbandman, obey the control of the intelligent and strenuous. The order is rigid. There is an awful sternness in its certainty; but it grows benign to him who has mastered its secret. It obeys him as a servant, it helps him as a friend; and the certainty with which he can calculate its action is one essential element of its friendliness. If he could not weigh the materials and measure the forces which are constantly around him, if he could not count on their known relations and actions with the same calm certainty with which he expects the

sunrise to light him to his daily toils, his life would be one of miserable dependence; he would live the serf of nature, and not her king. It is the unalterable fixity of relations and forces which God has given him the power to discover and to employ, which constitutes the royalty of his rule over nature; if that be destroyed or shaken, his crown rolls in the dust. The constancy of the relations and forces of the universe, their impassibility to the force which man's will can bring to bear upon them, of which his husbandry gives him full experience, is an essential element, perhaps we might say *the* essential element, in that higher culture which they offer to his spirit; it is this which makes the life of even the workman something higher than a lottery, and the toils of earth an education for the works and the joys of heaven.

3. The writer of this book, while he sees this grand, calm, and constant order very clearly, and appreciates its ministry to man, has a dark, sad vision of the uncertainties which cross it—the strength and magnitude of the variable element in nature and in life, which perplexes and baffles the strenuous workman, keeps him constantly on the tenter-hooks of anxiety, and not seldom rends his heart with anguish, and lays his fairest and proudest achievements in ruins in the dust. A certain order is there, all men can see it. Yes, men say,—and especially orientals, in whose climate the destructive agencies often run riot; but there is a dire disorder, and the disorder triumphs. Who knows the pathway of the storms, the earthquakes, the lava floods, the drought, and the deluge? who knows and rules their times? The fairest homesteads are made desolate in a moment; verdant beauty as of Eden vanishes, and blasting and burning as of Sodom reigns in its room. There are malign powers in the universe which seem to watch all beauty and increase, that they may make it their prey. Do not men in all ages tremble as they rejoice in prosperity? Do not the proverbs of all nations warn us that trouble in such moments is near? There is a hand unseen which deals destruction to our harvests and home-

steads, in the moment when they smile on us most gaily; and we are powerless to resist it; we can but sit like Job on the dunghill of our ruined fortunes and bemoan ourselves, and it may be curse the day which sent us forth to till such a treacherous seed-field as this. The dearest things, the things which we love most tenderly, the possession of which is our life, may be struck down in a moment, the delight of our eyes laid low at a stroke; we may plead and pray, we may wrestle with God in a frenzy of supplication: the hand which grasps our treasure is pitiless; pass a few days, we shall be standing tearless and defiant by the grave of our beloved. Pagans exclaim against their gods as treacherous, and refuse them service. Catholics revenge themselves by cashiering their saint. Nay, the same brutal instinct may be found in Protestant England: I have heard of a farmer, whose harvest was all ruined, sticking a rotten sheaf in the hedge and leaving it there, to make, as he said, God Almighty ashamed. We shudder at the blasphemy; but it is only a coarse expression of the anguish of the helpless in the hand of a power which seems inexorable and merciless, which crosses their most settled purposes, destroys ruthlessly their most precious harvests, and murders all their brightest joys. "*If the clouds be full of rain, they empty themselves upon the earth: and if the tree fall toward the south, or toward the north, in the place where the tree falleth, there it shall be. He that observeth the wind shall not sow; and he that regardeth the clouds shall not reap. As thou knowest not what is the way of the spirit, nor how the bones do grow in the womb of her that is with child: even so thou knowest not the works of God who maketh all. In the morning sow thy seed, and in the evening withhold not thine hand: for thou knowest not whether shall prosper, either this or that, or whether they both shall be alike good*" (ver. 3–6). There is a power at work behind the veil which may at any moment cross our purpose by some unexpected stroke, which gives to us no account of its methods, and which allows no court of appeal from its decrees. The tree falls, and who can foresee when it may fall? And when it falls, it cares not what it crushes, and the wrecks of it strew our fairest fields, and bury our golden harvests in the dust.

III. What then? There being this law of calamity at work, defying all calculation and all defence, what is the true policy of life?

There are mainly two policies of life; the stoic and the Christian. The Stoic says,—Everything is beyond my control, but myself. There is a kingdom whose sceptre can never be wrested from my hand. *Things* are certain enemies of my peace. I will make myself independent of *things*. I will reduce my relations with things outside me to a minimum. I am surer of a crust than of a banquet; so I will train myself to care only for a crust; a crust of food, a crust of wealth, a crust of friendship will be enough for me. I will fold the cloak of my manhood around me, and shake myself free of all dependence on fickle fortune and mortal friends.

The Christian says,—Everything is beyond my control, but myself. So far, he and the Stoic are at one. But he reflects that what is beyond HIS control is not beyond all control. This law of calamity obeys the rule of One who has given the most solemn and awful pledge that He loves me as a friend and treats me as a child. He would not have me adopt the demeanour and policy of an outcast in a storm, but of a child at home. I will throw my nature open to the sunlight. I will make myself as rich as possible in all good and beautiful possessions, and in troops of friends. It is the will of Him who rules my life that I should be so; He made me with all these affections and sympathies; He made me to feel life a blessing. I will work and be glad, and live and love according to His will; and trust, not my own hardness, but my Father's mercy, to spare me over-much pain, and to make life in some due measure a joy. Here are the two policies. How does the text decide? "*Cast thy bread upon the waters: for thou shalt find it after many days.*" "*If the clouds be full of rain, they empty themselves upon the earth: and if the tree fall toward the south, or toward the north, in the place where the tree falleth, there it shall be." "In the morning sow thy seed, and in the evening withhold not thine hand: for thou knowest not whether shall prosper, either this or that, or whether they both shall be alike good."* The argument is, God who made you to toil, to till the ground, and to till the more difficult and perilous seed-field of domestic, social, and political life, made the world thus. Both your vocation as a workman, and the field of your labour, with the conditions of that labour, are ordained by Him. There must then be an essential harmony. One wise and intelligent Being as the author of the whole system; and this law of calamity is not at war with your vocation, but is also its minister, and in deep and far-reaching ways is working with you to your ends. It is not, according to the dark pagan theory, the work of a malign spirit, strong enough to break in and make the homesteads and the lives which God has made His charge, a wreck. *"I form the light and create darkness; I make peace and create evil; I, the Lord, do all these things."* It is all the work of one hand, and that a wise and loving one. Work on, work bravely, work gaily; storms may sweep your fields and shadows may darken your homes; but no calamity, inward or outward, is unto death. The storm and blight of this year will swell the bulk of next year's harvests; and the deeper cares and sorrows of our spiritual husbandry but load us with an increase which the years lay up in the garners of eternity. Practically, the husbandman finds it to be so. Making the fullest allowance for all the crosses, the storms, the blights, the violence of Nature and of man, the balance is still amply on the side of the faithful workman. Year by year man's tillage advances; the wilderness and the solitary place is made glad by his toil, and the desert rejoices and blossoms as the rose. This means that a wise and loving Hand holds all the disturbing forces under control, and fixes their bounds where they instruct and stimulate, but never on a grand scale scare and paralyse mankind. The losses and the crosses of the croupier of the gaming table are borne with profound patience, for there is a certain chance in his favour which must inevitably in the long run fill his coffers with gain. How calmly, how joyously, should *we* work on through our storms and sorrows, who have, not a margin of security guaranteed by the theory of probabilities, but the certainty of an abundant and glorious harvest, if we are faithful and patient, guaranteed by the living God.

And do not pervert the teaching of the Scripture by narrowing its scope. It does not say,—Work, for the work is good for you; results are nothing. It says rather,—Work, for God is working with you, and results are His care. The Lord does not say,—Take no thought for the morrow, for these cares of food and clothes and health are sordid; despise them, and think exclusively of higher things. Quite other, and infinitely more wise and tender, is His teaching,—Do not be distracted by cares, "*for your heavenly Father knoweth that ye have need of all these things*," and how He furnishes those who trust Him let the birds and the lilies declare. "*Cast thy bread upon the waters*," for there is One watching it who will bring it back after many days. "*They that sow in tears shall reap in joy.*" "*He that goeth forth and weepeth, bearing precious seed, shall doubtless*"—doubtless because the Lord of the harvest assures it—"*come again with rejoicing, bringing his sheaves with him.*"

Three practical principles, which indicate the Christian policy of life, I gather from the text:—

1. Do not be afraid of giving with bountiful hand lest your charity should be wasted. Scatter your gifts freely: "*freely ye have received, freely give.* "*He that hath a bountiful eye shall be blessed*," blessed with the blessedness of Christ, and like Christ he shall gather in rich harvests. Sow your gifts as the husbandman scatters the seed in his furrows, leaving it with God to watch it, to bless its springing, to ripen its fruit. Much of our charity, our

effort to bless mankind, must seem to be futile. The waters close on it, it vanishes from sight and touch, it is rotting, we think, in the depths. No; I think that the discovery of the unknown fruit of the patient efforts and the loving sacrifices for men which on earth seemed to us to be wasted, will be one of the purest and intensest joys of eternity.

2. Do not be afraid of working lest your toil should be fruitless. There is no fruitless labour. Every hammer-stroke on the forge of duty welds something which will outlast eternity. Work with a will then, with a courage, an energy, a hope, to which Heaven lends its inspiration; and believe that nothing is so sure in the universe as your harvest. This seed of your toil may be stolen, that may be crushed, that may be blighted when it is set for fruit; but the grand sum of your labour is beyond the reach of the Harpies. God guards it, God quickens it, and God and angels will rejoice with you when one day you bring your golden harvest home.

3. Do not be afraid of loving because every love is a sure germ of pain. Throw wide the doors of your heart to all comers in the name of the Lord. The sorrows will spring, but the joys will overflow them. Count yourself rich, as you are rich in love. Keen sorrow it must bring, but with it superabounding joy. Ask God to hallow your loves, and to consecrate your crosses, and the pain is purged of all its bitterness; it is but the first throb of a great unspeakable joy, which will play like sunlight around your life in the homes where the weary are for ever at rest.

V.

THE LOST BIRTHRIGHT.

"Esau, who for one morsel of meat sold his birthright. For ye know how that afterward, when he would have inherited the blessing, he was rejected: for he found no place of repentance, though he sought it carefully with tears."—HEB. xii. 16, 17.

THESE words have always seemed to be among the very saddest in the book of God. No place of repentance, though sought carefully with tears! It is a very terrible picture, and seems to describe the experience of what must have been a very wretched and blighted life. It is possible that if we study the matter closely some of the tones of sadness may be lightened; but still Esau and his sad history will remain one of the dark perplexities of Scripture, just as the acts and the fate of men like Esau are among the most inscrutable mysteries of life. There are men like Esau cropping up everywhere; men who seem born to lose their birthright, to be befooled by the keen and subtle Jacobs, to be seeking ever places of repentance, and to find Fate inexorable to their tears. Men *born* under the dark doom of the rejected, we are tempted to say—so inevitable their destiny appears from the first. In this case, "*the elder shall serve the younger,*" was written of the twin brethren in the womb, and Jacob was the successful supplanter from his birth. There are many sad mysteries in life, and the history of such natures and their destiny are among the saddest. We cannot hope to fathom it on earth; but blessed be God for the assurance which we are not only permitted but bound to cherish, that all which is inscrutable here and dark with shadows will unfold a divine order and beauty in the long bright day of eternity.

Esau and Jacob, both in their personal character and

their relations with each other, are representative men, and foreshow in brief the essential character of large phases and long periods of human development. They place before us, as we read the record of their personal history, the great twin brethren, the Gentile and the Jewish, perhaps even more widely the Christian and the heathen, sections of mankind. The earlier records of the book of God are full of such typical characters and lives. In truth, in the earliest time life was typical; men lived in large and free intercourse with Nature and with their fellow-men. The conventional swathing-bands with which modern society has bound itself were unknown. Men lived boldly from within, and what they said and did had broad human significance, and forecast naturally what men would say and do under the same conditions to the end of time. Hence, we imagine, the exceeding fulness of the book of Genesis in its painting of character and life. Nowhere have we anything like such large and graphic portraiture as here. The reason is surely that in those ages life was richly doctrinal, and that the God who caused all Holy Scripture to be written for our learning saw that the history of such lives as those of Abraham, Isaac, Esau, Jacob, and Joseph, would be the most precious legacy which could be handed down from the age of the patriarchs to all time.

The contrast of these two men is peculiarly rich and instructive. Esau is the lusty, genial, jovial pagan; impulsive, impetuous, frank, and generous, but sensual and self-willed. A man keenly alive to the claims and experiences of the moment; slow to believe in unseen realities and the harvest which could only be reaped beyond long years of patience and pain. Jacob, on the other hand, led from the first a meditative and interior life. What may be meant by the description, "a plain man, dwelling in tents," is not very apparent. It certainly does not simply describe a fact in his history, but rather a feature of his character. He loved the home life; while the burly Esau was abroad in the field, he loved to sit at home, meditating on many things, and amongst them the highest—a plain man, sound, pure, pious, as some commentators have it. The meaning of the word is certainly moral; "*integer vitæ*" may perhaps express it. The pilgrim Abraham was reproduced in Jacob in some of the main features of his character. He could understand, at any rate, what Esau apparently could never understand—the sacredness of a Divine vocation, the value of a birthright which carried with it a Divine benediction, and which was freighted with the Divine promise to the world. The grand distinction between the two men from the first was, that Jacob had faith, while Esau had none. Jacob had the heart of a pilgrim, Esau the heart of a "prince of this world." Jacob saw something behind the veil, which filled his soul with awe and made his life a constant aspiration; Esau saw that on this side the veil which filled him with the only pleasure which he cared to grasp at, and which taught him to look upon his brother's pilgrim lot and halting step as the sign of a broken and wasted life. Esau had his grand success in the princedom which he founded. You may read the list of the "dukes of Edom, who sprang from him," in the chapters which record his history. The sad and weary Jacob, standing before Pharaoh when his race was well nigh run, witnessed this confession, "*Few and evil have the days of the years of my life been, and have not attained unto the days of the years of the life of my fathers in the days of their pilgrimage.*" His success lay beyond generations and ages, beyond the rising of the "Star that should come out of" his house, beyond the resurrection day. Jacob's life won no success but such as he shares with humanity in time and in eternity. His success is our success; in his blessing we are blessed. He stands forth in the early twilight of history as the typical child of the kingdom, the Prince of God, having power with two worlds. He is the representative of the elect men and races. This election is a broad, plain, principle of God's government. In all ages God is wont to call men, races, nations, out of the commonwealth of humanity, and to bring them near unto Himself. Their election is to service—high service, hard battle, stern endurance. First in honour, they must be first in perils, pains, temptations, and toils. Privilege is a word of abundant meaning in the book of God's dispensations; but it means privilege to be first—to lead the van, to clear the way, to open new paths for progress through the jungle of ignorance and night. Privilege to belong to a privileged class, to special advantage and certain success; privilege to run the race of life, light and trim against weighted competitors, is part of the devil's gospel, not of God's. Of this royal class, who are God's elect ministers to mankind in all their generations, Jacob is a typical representative. We learn from his character and history what God means by callings, birthrights, and blessings, and how much those whom He places in the front rank have to toil and suffer for the world. There is something in Jacob's character and in the development of his life which is significant for all time, which forecasts the course of Jewish and Christian ages, and prophesies in broad outline the method of God's universal culture of our race.

At the same time the patriarch of Israel presents to us a wonderfully complete image of the race which sprang from him. We speak of Jacob rather than Abraham, as the founder of the people to which he gave his name; Abraham, the father of the faithful, is the founder of a yet richer and mightier line. But Jacob is the typical Jew. His life, like the life of his people, is simply incomprehensible to those who cannot realize a Divine vocation, who cannot cling to a Divine promise, who cannot struggle and suffer in faith for the sake of far-off divine results, whereby humanity at large would be blessed. Jacob's life was made what it was by the commerce which he held with the unseen God of his fathers. They have but a dim eye for the meaning of history who cannot see that, under all this man's questionable deeds and chequered experience, this faith in God was the deepest and strongest element in his nature. It ruled the critical moments of his life, it sustained him through all the stormiest scenes of his pilgrimage, and it shone out clearest and strongest in death. Scarcely had he gone forth an exile from the house of his fathers, when this fruitful commerce with God and the spiritual world was established. The beautiful narrative in Genesis casts a flood of light on his life. "*And Jacob went out from Beersheba, and went toward Haran. And he lighted upon a certain place, and tarried there all night, because the sun was set; and he took of the stones of that place and put them for his pillows, and lay down in that place to sleep. And he dreamed, and behold, a ladder set up on the earth, and the top of it reached to heaven: and, behold, the angels of God ascending and descending on it. And, behold, the Lord stood above it, and said, I am the Lord God of Abraham thy father, and the God of Isaac: the land whereon thou liest, to thee will I give it, and to thy seed; and thy seed shall be as the dust of the earth, and thou shalt spread abroad to the west, and to the east, and to the north, and to the south: and in thee and in thy seed shall all the families of the earth be blessed. And, behold, I am with thee, and will keep thee in all places whither thou goest, and will bring thee again into this land: for I will not leave thee, until I have done that which I have spoken to thee of. And Jacob awaked out of his sleep, and he said, Surely the Lord is in this place, and I knew it not. And he was afraid, and said, How dreadful is this place! this is none other but the house of God, and this is the gate of heaven.*" (Gen. xxviii. 10–17.)

Precisely the same influence was formative of the character and destinies of his race. This high and grand quality, this openness to the influence of the "powers of the world to come," which is surely the grandest of all qualities, renders the highest Divine culture possible, with eternally blessed and glorious results. But it was marred and debased both in Jacob and in his people by the alloy of selfish, base, and carnal elements, of the earth earthy, which it was the great aim of all the Divine discipline under which he and his people suffered so sharply, to purge away and to destroy. And herein he represents a wider family than Israel. This Divine tincture, in a measure, is in all of us, mixed with the baser earthy matter. God's chosen ones, the subjects of His highest culture in all ages, have mostly the earthy element in full force, struggling with the Divine. No model men were the chosen people of ancient times, nor the saints of apostolic days. The one question is, Hast thou faith? *"Lord, I believe, help Thou mine unbelief,"* is substantially the confession of Jacob, of Israel, and of all who in any age form part of the Church of the living God. When Jacob, when the Jews, suffered themselves to forget the Divinity which was with them, which was *in* them, their superior power revealed itself as simply masterly craft. Jacob, viewed in one light, is just the most accomplished and successful schemer of his times; in another light, he is the grandest spiritual prince. His people repeat the anomaly. The race of the grandest spiritual power, of the most intense religious belief, have earned the character of the most accomplished hucksters and tricksters of the world. The power capable of the one, under the true inspiration, without it sank easily to the level of the other. There is a modern instance remarkably in point. In many respects the Scotch have succeeded to the character and position which the Jews occupied in ancient society. In both people there is the same grand spiritual power, the same prophetic spirit—Edward Irving was more after the fashion of an old Jewish prophet than any man, except perhaps Savonarola, whom we have had among us in these modern days—the same intense religious zeal, the same heroism in fighting and suffering for their faith, mixed up with the same worldly ambition, the same cautious and canny temper, the same facility of dispersion, and the same power of getting on and winning wealth and influence wherever

God might cast their lot. Is there not a manifestation of the same law in the history of the universal Church? As with Jacob, as in Judaism, so in Christendom, the leading spiritual magnates, the prominent Churchmen of all ages, forsaking their true strength, divesting themselves of their true power as Christ's priests and kings, have sunk to the level of the most selfish schemers, and have won the reputation of the cleverest and wiliest statesmen of the world. Churchcraft in all ages has been held to be a shade more worldly, more subtle, more ruthless, than statecraft. The old proverb, "the corruption of the best is the worst" partly accounts for it; but something is due also to the principle whose workings we trace through Jacob's history, that the power which, inspired of God, is capable of Godlike activity, when the world or the devil get hold of it, is capable of all manner of worldly and devilish work with fell energy and success.

But Jacob's life was purified and elevated as it passed through its tremendous discipline. The aged pilgrim, having won the title of Prince of God, stood before Pharaoh clothed with a dignity and power which made the world's mightiest monarch bend eagerly under the blessing of his hand. "*The Angel which redeemed me from all evil,*" he spake of, when his eyes were growing dim in death. The history of his life is the history of that redemption, and this is its rich meaning for us. He sinned basely and shamefully, he suffered as few have suffered, and wrestled as few have strength to wrestle for the blessing which purified and redeemed his life. A sad, stricken, broken man, halting painfully on his thigh, he went on his way, but ennobled, purified, and saved. His life is a revelation of the way of God in the discipline of our spirits; how power gets educated and purified, and made meet at last for the work and the joy of eternity. So Judaism, as it struggled on and suffered, lost some of its baser elements, and came forth, developed, into a higher region of experience and power, in the life of the Christian Church.

The study of the character of these two men is full of the richest interest and instruction; but our present purpose is with the elder, and this profoundly sad passage of his history. There is much, in the matter of both the birthright and the repentance of which our text speaks, which is frequently very grievously and even disastrously misunderstood, which is supposed to present ideas of the dealings of God with man which contradict the fundamental principles of the gospel, and casts no trifling stumbling-blocks before the steps of faith. That we may understand it truly let us consider—

I. That the rejection of the elder, and the election of the younger to honour and power—to all that the election of God could bring—by no means stands by itself in the history of the Divine dispensations; and it illustrates an important principle on which we will dwell for a moment before we pass on.

We are tempted to think that, on the whole, Esau was a hardly used man, and that we have here an instance of the exercise of the Divine sovereignty which is harsh, arbitrary, and unjust. In the natural course of things, Esau would have had the birthright and all that it was worth. It is made to appear that by a purely arbitrary act Esau was robbed of it, while Jacob was endowed with it, having no sort of superior claim. Paul, in Romans ix. 10-13, is careful to insist that whatever the principle may be which is at work here, at any rate it is not merit, for the decree was pronounced long before any questions of merit could have force. The sovereignty of God is here the keystone of his argument: it is worth our while to discern, as far as we may, the reason on which this act of sovereignty rests. Of course the sympathy which we extend to Esau is based upon some idea of the rights of the elder born which seems to be instinctive in the human heart. This opens a wide question into which we have no need in this place to enter. The principle is recognised plainly enough in the word of God. In Deuteronomy xxi. 15-17, there is explicit legislation on the subject. "*If a man have two wives, one beloved, and another hated, and they have born him children, both the beloved and the hated; and if the firstborn son be her's that was hated: then it shall be, when he maketh his sons to inherit that which he hath, that he may not make the son of the beloved firstborn before the son of the hated, which is indeed the firstborn: but he shall acknowledge the son of the hated for the firstborn, by giving him a double portion of all that he hath: for he is the beginning of his strength; the right of the firstborn is his.*" Joseph was evidently grieved when Jacob blessed the younger with the blessing of the firstborn, as though some sacred order had been violated: and the very word "firstborn" is employed as a term of dignity and pre-eminence both in the Old and the New Testament scriptures. I believe it to be for the good of society that this order should exist; that the eldest son should be looked upon as the representative of the family, while the younger sons should regard it as their lot—and not the worse lot in the sight of God and the angels—to carve out a new fortune for themselves. I believe this to be a Divine institution, and that God contemplated it when he established the family life as the basis of human society. But just because it is an order ordained of God, man shall not make an idol of it. A certain free play in the working of an order or an institution is essential to the well-being and progress of society. If God had so ordered all the dispensations, that the elder son was constituted invariably the organ of His communication with the household, the tribe, the race, it would have instituted a caste instead of a principle of order, and the great majority of our race would, in that case, be outcast from their birth. That this rule of the elder might not become a tyrannous thing, that the younger sons of the house might feel that they too had a man's part to play on the theatre of life, a part which might easily become grander and more glorious than that of the firstborn, God, at great critical moments, seems to have broken through the order, and made the younger the heir of the promises and the organ of His revelation to mankind. Jacob is a notable, a typical instance. The case of David is hardly less remarkable, 1 Sam. xvi. 6-13. And Paul in the spiritual family illustrates the same principle; the youngest born of the apostles, one in his own estimation hardly meet to be called an apostle, laboured more abundantly than they all, and was crowned with the most glorious success. But these arbitrary selections, as they appear at first sight, in reality, when we look more closely, are found to deliver the institution of primogeniture from arbitrariness; and they show to us that the Will which rules the world maintains its freedom under the guidance of its wisdom, and remits to no institution, however useful or honourable, the supreme power in the conduct of human affairs. It seems as though, knowing man's inherent propensity to formalism, the Lord had visibly broken through, from time to time, the very forms which He had Himself established, that He might show decisively that forms can have noble use alone in the hands of the free. Two singular instances of this, closely parallel to each other, are to be found in the numbers of the tribes of Israel and of the apostles of Christ. We talk familiarly of twelve tribes and of twelve apostles. But were there truly twelve or thirteen in each case? The question is by no means easy to answer. The tribe of Joseph was split into two. Theoretically, it is easy to regard the tribes of Ephraim and Manasseh as forming together the one tribe of Joseph. But, practically, we must remember that the tribe of Ephraim was the most powerful and masterful of the tribes until the rise of the house of David. If any tribe might be looked upon as complete, certainly it would be the tribe of Ephraim. So that, looking at it in the light of actual history, we should be compelled to reckon thirteen, but for the fact that the separation of the tribe of Levi for the priesthood reduced to twelve the number of tribes claiming tribal settlement in Canaan, and active in the spheres of industry, politics, and war. Similarly, it is an open question how far the place of Judas among the Twelve was lawfully filled up by the election of Matthias. It is far from clear that Peter and the infant Church were not acting hastily in this election and ordination of a successor to the apostate. We hear the name of Matthias only, and then he disappears from history. While we soon meet with an apostle of the Lord's election, who, if Matthias was duly called, raises the number of the apostles to thirteen. Is not this uncertainty, this fringe of doubt, left hanging around the numbers in these important and critical instances with a set purpose, that men might not make an idol of the number? That men might not think in the one case that the firstborn were the world's sole masters, nor dream in the other that a college of twelve was essential to the conduct of all the great spiritual movements of mankind.

II. The question of the birthright seems to us to be one on which there is, popularly at any rate, a good deal of misunderstanding. We will look at it a little more closely, before we proceed to consider the unavailing repentance which will form the topic of a second discourse.

There is something which reaches beyond the merely historico-representative character, in the history of these twain. Most of the earnest and generous students of the Old Testament would, we imagine, if they were to make frank confession, sympathise with Esau as a wronged and ill-used man. A sentiment of pity for the big, burly hunter, so helpless in the hands of the subtle and masterly Jacob, takes possession of us as we read the history. It seems a hard penalty to pay for a moment's weakness under the pressure of the pangs of hunger; while the crafty treacherous falsehood by which the blessing as well as the birthright was won from him enlists us wholly as to that transaction on his side. This sentiment of compassion is much strengthened by the vague impression that, through the craft of Jacob, Esau suffered a terrible and irreparable loss. And younger sons, as they see the paternal acres, the family mansion, and the dignity of the family name, passing to the elder, are prone to make the same moan, and to reckon themselves the predestined victims of the social order of the world. Learn from this history how the matter really stands. Esau had all the birthright which he honestly cared for; while Jacob had simply that birthright which, blessed be Christ, is within reach of every child of every household upon earth. Do not waste your pity upon Esau, on the ground of what he lost. Pity him rather on the score of what he did not care to win. It would be a great mistake to suppose that Jacob's treachery left the elder brother a broken and ruined man; on the contrary, the ruin in the worldly sense fell on the man who won the birthright; and though the blessing was added, he went a broken and halting man to the end of his days. That exceeding great and bitter cry, which was wrung from the disinherited when he saw the paternal blessing following the birthright, did not continue to wail through his life. He was a warm-hearted, loving, and generous man, though of fiery passion. The loss of the good old Isaac's benediction struck him to the heart; but we are wrong in supposing that it remained a burden on his life. Nothing of the kind; it had been better for him if it had been so. But the fury seems soon to have passed away, probably too his regrets. He became a chieftain of wealth and renown, rich, strong, illustrious. We meet with him again, and there is no trace of a shadow over his life. "*And Jacob lifted up his eyes, and looked, and, behold, Esau came, and with him four hundred men. And he divided the children unto Leah, and unto Rachel, and unto the two handmaids. And he put the handmaids and their children foremost, and Leah and her children after, and Rachel and Joseph hindermost. And he passed over before them, and bowed himself to the ground seven times, until he came near to his brother. And Esau ran to meet him, and embraced him, and fell on his neck, and kissed him: and they wept. And he lifted up his eyes, and saw the women and the children; and said, Who are those with thee?*

And he said, The children which God hath graciously given thy servant. Then the handmaidens came near, they and their children, and they bowed themselves. And Leah also with her children came near, and bowed themselves: and after came Joseph near and Rachel, and they bowed themselves. And he said, What meanest thou by all this drove which I met? And he said, These are to find grace in the sight of my lord. And Esau said, I have enough, my brother; keep that thou hast unto thyself." (Gen. xxxiii. 1–9.) "*And Esau took his wives, and his sons, and his daughters, and all the persons of his house, and his cattle, and all his beasts, and all his substance, which he had got in the land of Canaan; and went into the country from the face of his brother Jacob. For their riches were more than that they might dwell together; and the land wherein they were strangers could not bear them, because of their cattle. Thus dwelt Esau in mount Seir. Esau is Edom."* (Gen. xxxvi. 6–8.) Read the catalogue of his princely descendants, and remember that Edom played a splendid part in the political, and especially the commercial, history of the oriental world. Esau lost that, and that alone, which his soul had no love for, and no power to use to honour. But he won that in which his soul delighted; he passed a lifetime of splendid and careless prosperity, and in a good old age went down to his grave in peace.

And what did Jacob win by his birthright—his rights of the firstborn? Simply the power to become God's pilgrim, the power to win a lofty height of honour and renown by life-long patience, by heroic struggle, by wearing, wasting toils. What good shall this birthright do to me, said the hungry hunter, mad for the mess of pottage which the thrifty Jacob sold. But what good did the birthright do to the supplanter who bought it, and filched the blessing with it? None, absolutely none, in the sense in which they talk of "good" who are reckoning gains. It drove him forth from the very hour when he stole his father's blessing, an exile to a distant land. It made him for long years, his best years, a hireling in his kinsman's house. It exposed him to precisely the kind of trick which he himself had practised, in a matter of yet deeper moment to his affection; for it imperilled the winning of the woman whom he tenderly loved. After he had served for long years as a hireling for a hireling's wage, it brought him back at length to the threshold of the promised Canaan. Rich in the wealth of the East, he drew near the borders. His soul was filled with perturbation when he heard that Esau was coming to meet him. The wrong which his brother had suffered rose up freshly before him in all its disgraceful features, and he could hardly believe in the hunter's generous forgiveness as he cowered a suppliant at his feet. Entered at length on the land of his inheritance, discord breaks out in his home and embitters his life. He is struck to the heart through his dearest affections. "There I buried Rachel" is the epitaph of a great agony; and when Joseph was not, he felt that he should go down mourning to the grave. At length the land of his inheritance refused to sustain him; and the weary old pilgrim, with one foot in the grave, goes forth once more an exile—the second and final exile—into a land where the sons for whom he won and held the birthright were destined for centuries to writhe and moan as slaves. What good did the birthright do to him?

If you look at the things which are seen, which are mostly in view when birthrights are in question, Esau, the hardly used man, the victim, had most unquestionably the preferable lot. The time came when he stood as a prince before Jacob, and Jacob bowed himself at his feet. There was no malignant spirit at work here, as we are sometimes tempted to conceive of it, making Esau's life wretched and broken, while Jacob's was heaped high with all which could gladden a grasping and sensual heart; on the contrary, the chosen son won only that which Esau would not have cared to lift if it had been laid at his very feet. Esau lost only that which would have been life-long a torment to his easy, jovial, sensual nature, which he would have prayed to get rid of, which he would in some way have got rid of, if it had clung to him, no matter at what cost. There were some, remember, who, finding their herds of swine in peril, prayed even the merciful Saviour "to depart out of their coasts." Jacob seized a bitter inheritance as far as this world was concerned, by his clever impersonation; while Rebekah, who prompted and managed it, paid a yet heavier price for it; in this world she never saw her darling more.

What he won was power with God and with man as a spiritual prince; power to pray, and to conquer by prayer; power to trust and to hope in God's mercy through stern struggles and bitter miseries; and power to reach a hand through death and lay up the hope of his soul with God on high. The heart which could crave for a spiritual thing, which pined to be a child of promise, which clung to the traditions of his fathers and the hope of his house, all which Esau scorned, God trained by suffering to aim continually at higher and yet higher things. He won, in a word, a high place in God's high school of discipline, and a name of renown as a spiritual hero in time and in eternity. This was practically his gain; and it is precisely this which God places fairly within your reach. You too may be the sons of promise; "power to become the sons of God" is the birthright which in Christ is yours. Jacob, no doubt, and most justly, seems to you the grander man as compared with Esau, and his life the nobler and more glorious life. Then live it. All that he won you may win. Make yourself a prince of God by wrestling prayer. The birthright of broad acres and family honours may pass to your elder. The birthright of hard work, stern struggle, strong effort, high aspiration, disciplined power, victorious faith, eternal renown and joy, is yours. Christ has won it, and freely bestows it—no younger son's portion, but the birthright of the eldest, the only-begotten son, glorious through time and eternity. It may be that many a younger son may read these words; many a one who may be tempted to bemoan himself that the younger son's portion, the lot of toil and struggle, has fallen to him in life. Well! if it be so, bless God for it. If the lot of the younger be toil and struggle, if it falls to them mainly to open new paths, not without peril and pain, to win by earnest and patient effort strength and wisdom, and to take the leader's place in the battle-field of life, don't moan over it if it has fallen to you, but again I say bless God for it. The nobler, the richer, the lordlier inheritance, is yours. Pity, do not despise, but pity the elders who sit clothed in purple and fine linen, faring sumptuously every day. It would be a strange history if it were fairly written out, the history of younger sons, with a just estimate of what they have done in comparison with the elder for the service and progress of mankind. The eldest born, the heirs, with the inheritance which the past has lazily left to them; the younger sons, with the domain of wisdom, strength, and influence, which their own right hand, God helping them, has won. If Jacob seems to you the petted child of fortune, the chosen favourite of heaven, and Esau the wretched reprobate outcast, spurned alike of man and of God, then take Jacob's inheritance; take it, it is fairly yours. Spurn Esau's, which the devil is putting into your hand. Be your choice the pilgrim's toils and struggles, the name of renown, the everlasting portion; and with the words of the pilgrim's hymn upon your lips pass on your way.

"Contented now upon my thigh
  I halt, till life's short journey end;
All helplessness, all weakness, I
  On Thee alone for strength depend;
Nor have I power from Thee to move;
Thy nature and Thy name is Love.

Lame as I am, I take the prey;
  Hell, earth, and sin, with ease o'ercome;
I leap for joy, pursue my way,
  And, as a bounding hart, fly home;
Through all eternity to prove
Thy nature and Thy name is Love."

VI.

NO PLACE OF REPENTANCE.

"He found no place of repentance, though he sought it carefully with tears."—HEB. xii. 17.

WE have shown in the last discourse that a close examination of the question of the birthright lightens some of the deeper shadows which lie upon it. Comparing the outward and visible aspect of the two men—the man who sold the birthright and lost the blessing, and the man who won them both—it would appear that the balance of worldly prosperity was altogether on Esau's side. Esau lost just that which his soul despised, and he won what his soul lusted after, wealth, power, and the position of a prince. He lived prosperously and splendidly, and died peacefully we may believe, with few regrets. There is certainly nothing in the few words which are devoted to his subsequent history to suggest that he lived a disappointed ruined man. On the contrary, he seems to have displayed on his meeting with Jacob that magnanimity and generosity which shallow natures are wont to manifest in a prosperous lot. It is just the glow of the sunlight reflected from their lives: the rippling shallows make a braver show in the sunlight than the still deep pools; and Esaus are gayer objects to look at, when all goes well with them, than the careworn halting pilgrim, who bears on his brow, and no sunlight can efface it, the marks of many toils and tears. But be that as it may, there can be no question that the Bible does not picture the life of Esau as a broken and ruined life, as far as this world is concerned. The man grew rich and powerful, so rich that he could afford to make light of Jacob's presents, so powerful that Jacob's company was helpless in his hand. It is written that once the children of Israel cried for flesh, and "*God gave them flesh, but sent leanness into their souls.*" Something like this was the history of Esau, and of how many a worldly-hearted man whom fortune loads with gifts, while the springs of his higher life sink low and die. And his race prospered. As Jacob was to Esau, quite the weaker and more dependent of the two, so when centuries passed was Israel to Edom. The descendants of Esau had attained to such strength and political influence that they were able to bar the gates of their land against the elect host, pilgrims through the wilderness like their sire, angel-led, and saved by hope. On the whole then, for himself and his descendants, his life must be pronounced a worldly success.

Jacob, on the other hand, had to reap life-long the bitter fruits of his craft and fraud. His life was a weary, wasting struggle with selfish craft and evil passion in all who surrounded him. He spent the best years of his life in exile, and stood before Pharaoh, in his own judgment prematurely aged and decayed. He won a name and a place which called him to submit to a searching discipline, to live the life of a pilgrim, to dwell as a stranger in his promised land, and to die in exile at last. The world was fuller to him of sorrows and toils than of benedictions, and the crown which the Prince of God at last was able to bind around his brow was set with many a thorn. But he won the power to follow the Angel, the Angel which redeemed him from all evil; his life, halting as was his step, was a noble spiritual progress from strength to strength, from victory to victory, till he passed up to receive the prize of his conflict in a world and from a hand which Esau "despised."

Looked at in the light of this world's interests then, some of the darkest difficulties vanish as we read the record of this birthright lost and won. But then there is Esau himself, the man who despised his birthright, who counted himself unworthy of the honour to which God had ordained him, incapable of the glorious toil and patience to which God had called him, and careless of the prize which God had placed within reach of his hand. The life of this man, from the higher point of view, was as sad, wretched, and faithless, as was the pilgrim Jacob's from the lower. He won his wealth and his princedom by his energy of hand and will in all things that pertained to this life; but he let all the interests and hopes of the higher life fade out of the horizon, and the crown of his spiritual manhood slip from the grasp of his careless hand. He touched it, but he could not hold it. What good shall this birthright do to me, he moaned when the mess of pottage steamed before his hungry senses; and the crown rolled in the dust. There is the man Esau, under all his possession and princedom, in the sight of God a very wretched and poverty-stricken outcast of the kingdom whose citizens believe in truth, duty, spiritual effort, conflict, prayer, self-sacrifice, heaven, and God. About the case of Esau personally there are many heavy difficulties. His course seems to have been in a measure marked out from his birth: "*The elder shall serve the younger*" was said of the twin brethren while they were yet in the womb: and some such relation of the two seems to be involved in the destiny which a higher Will had from the first decreed. And this opens the vision of an abyss of mystery, into the depths of which no finite intellect can search—the relation of connate constitution and temperament to character, and the measure in which this bears on the supreme fact of man's being, responsibility. Responsibility, implying freedom in the largest sense, we hold to be the corner stone of our dignity as men. If man be not free, with the everlasting crown of freedom within his reach as the prize of all his toils and struggles, why! there is not a cur that prowls about the streets whose lot is not more enviable. In that case man would be a combatant by a profound instinct of his nature, struggling sternly life-long against innumerable evils, with nothing after all to struggle for; pressed, crushed, by the weight of intolerable ills, with no hope to sanctify and no harvest to repay his pain. Who would not "rather be a dog and bay the moon," than such a creature? For freedom, and the responsibility which it brings, as the fundamental spiritual fact of our nature, we contend earnestly, yea vehemently, as for the only justification of God's constitution of the human world, the only key to the woes which He lets loose to afflict it and the discords with which He allows it to be torn. And for the reality of this moral freedom we shall have to do stern battle with the school who are urging now, with great subtilty and force, that all the moral phenomena of man's nature are just the finest efflorescence of the nerve matter of which his intelligence is manufactured, the cream of the milk of his natural law.

But it cannot be questioned for a moment that men appear to be under various conditions of advantage, as we might call it, with regard to the exercise of their freedom and its fruits. The differences arise partly, but not we believe chiefly, from circumstance. The child of a household of thieves or vagrants, for instance, seems to have but a poor chance in life compared with the children who grow up, pure, cultivated, comely, and pious, in your serene, happy, and orderly homes. But the more serious source of this inequality is to be found in character and temperament, inbred lusts, passions, tempers, and proclivities which may make the life of a man one long agony of struggle and failure, while another man more fairly endowed may find from the first the way of wisdom a way of pleasantness and all her paths paths of peace. A man born with a brutal nature and feeble spiritual energy, or with a native propensity, as far as we can see, to certain forms of sin—the temptation to which exercises the kind of fascination over his will which the serpent's eye is said to exert over the victim bird, but which another man would burst through as easily as Samson flung off the withes of the Philistine harlot—is, one is tempted to think, at a terrible disadvantage in life's battle, compared with the man who has a halo of saintly glory around his brow from his birth. It is a dark, sad mystery, much of which, after all our brooding over it, we must leave in trust with God.

I believe firmly that inequalities arising out of circumstances are after all far less real than they appear. The facilities and opportunities for a fair unfolding of life are not so uneven, in the various classes and callings, as they seem. There must be some deep meaning in the Saviour's words, "*Blessed are ye poor,*" and in the terrible sentence, "*How hardly shall they that have riches enter into the kingdom of God.*" There is an amount of practical Christianity—daily, hourly trust in God and ministry to each other—developed by the circumstances of the lot of the poor, which we may fairly set against the intelligent beliefs, the doctrinal correctness, and the measured charities of the richer class, as in the sight of God of equal or of higher price. There is nothing in a workman's lot or toil, to remove him farther from the gate of the kingdom than rich men, nobles, priests, or kings; nay, the balance is altogether in his favour. But, alas! there is a class far below the workman, a vast class, vastest in the great cities where Christian civilization is at the height of its splendour and power, whose lot it is terribly difficult to comprehend in a theodicy, and of whom it is hard to believe that they are not from the first at a fearful disadvantage as respects nearness to the gate of the kingdom of heaven. But the gravest side of the difficulty is not circumstantial; it concerns nature and temperament. Though perhaps, if we could search a little more deeply, we should see that each type of character has its own peculiar class of difficulties and temptations; and that the most beautiful and saintlike have their dread perils of shipwreck, which make their course as arduous as that of the souls which bear about with them a great load of fleshliness and groan under the bondage of tyrannous passions and lusts. Still it is a truth which is not without its awful significance, that temperaments, passions, and powers, are very variously distributed to men, while the burden of existence is laid equally upon all, and "every soul must bear its own burden" in time and in eternity.

These things lend infinite meaning to the word "Father" when uttered by Divine lips. Like as a father pitieth his children, the Father pitieth and beareth with us: "he knoweth our frame, he remembereth that we are dust." It is a father's compassion, tenderness, and equity which we need, to be the basis of our confidence and hope. A father considers with fatherly care, interest, and love our individual endowments, difficulties, and temptations, in ruling and in judging us; and He will ordain our eternal state with a merciful wisdom, which has to satisfy not a rigid justice only but the hopes and yearnings of a paternal heart. If it were not for the belief that the bar of judgment before which we shall stand is a wise and righteous fatherly heart, the best endowed might well faint under the burden of existence, while the worst would moan under its agony and curse the day on which they saw the sun. There are some very terrible sentences in the word of God, which utter the moan, not of the worst men, but of the best and noblest with whose history it deals. "*After this opened Job his mouth, and cursed his day. And Job spake, and said, Let the day perish wherein I was born, and the night in which it was said, There is a man child conceived. Let that day be darkness; let not God regard it from above, neither let the light shine upon it. Let darkness and the shadow of death stain it; let a cloud dwell upon it; let the blackness of the day terrify it. As for that night, let darkness seize upon it; let it not be joined unto the days of the year; let it not come into the number of the months. Lo, let that night be solitary, let no joyful voice come therein.*" (Job iii. 1–7.) "*Wherefore is light given to him that is in misery, and life unto the bitter in soul; Which long for death, but it cometh not: and dig for it more than for hid treasures; Which rejoice exceedingly, and are glad when they can find the grave? Why is light given to a man whose way is hid, and whom God hath hedged in? For my sighing cometh before I eat, and my roarings are poured out like the waters. For the thing which I greatly feared is come upon me, and that which I was afraid of is come unto me. I was not in safety, neither had I rest, neither was I quiet; yet trouble came."* (Job iii. 20–26.) *"Cursed be the day wherein I was born: let not the day wherein my mother bare me be blessed. Cursed be the man who brought tidings to my father, saying, A man child is born unto thee; making him very glad. And let that man be as the cities which the Lord overthrew, and repented not: and let him hear the cry in the morning, and the shouting at noontide. Because he slew me not from the womb; or that my mother might have been my grave, and her womb to be always great with me. Wherefore came I forth out of the womb to see labour and sorrow, that my days should be consumed with shame?"* (Jer. xx. 14–18.) These were not bad men, crushed under the burden of their own iniquity, but just, upright, and God-fearing men, who felt that existence was too terrible for them under conditions which hid from them the Father's ruling hand. And if they shrank from the burden of conscious responsible being, how shall weaker men escape its terror, but by taking refuge under the shield of a Father's equity and love! But these thoughts lend a most blessed meaning to the words of the Saviour: *"Then answered Jesus and said unto them, Verily, verily, I say unto you, The Son can do nothing of himself, but what he seeth the Father do: for what things soever he doeth, these also doeth the Son likewise. For the Father loveth the Son, and showeth him all things that himself doeth: and he will show him greater works than these, that ye may marvel. For as the Father raiseth up the dead, and quickeneth them; even so the Son quickeneth whom he will. For the Father judgeth no man, but hath committed all judgment unto the Son: That all men should honour the Son, even as they honour the Father. He that honoureth not the Son, honoureth not the Father which hath sent him. Verily, verily, I say unto you, He that heareth my word, and believeth on him that sent me, hath everlasting life, and shall not come into condemnation; but is passed from death unto life. Verily, verily, I say unto you, The hour is coming, and now is, when the dead shall hear the voice of the Son of God: and they that hear shall live. For as the Father hath life in himself; so hath he given to the Son to have life in himself; and hath given him authority to execute judgment also, because he is the Son of man."* (John v. 19–27.) "THE FATHER HATH COMMITTED ALL JUDGMENT UNTO THE SON." "BECAUSE HE IS THE SON OF MAN." Because He can take a man's measure as well as a Divine measure of a man's weaknesses, perils, and temptations; can measure, as a man, man's need of mercy, and utter the Divine Father's judgment from pitiful human lips. Few words, as we pore over these dark mysteries of existence, are so full of consolation and hope as these words of the Saviour upon judgment. We can bear the darkness, we can bear the anguish, if we are called to pass through it, because we know that the ordering of our destinies is in the hand of One who mingles with a brother's sympathy and tenderness the Divine Father's equity and love.

But the text does not touch upon these difficulties of Esau's history. It treats him broadly as the typical instance of the reprobate, the man who by his own base acts has cast himself out of the position for which he was born and trained; who by one decisive manifestation of his character and propensities has shut himself out from a high career which opened fairly before him, and who finds no means of reversing the decree which excludes him, though he seeks it carefully with tears. It opens a very terrible vision of the inexorable rigour with which deeds done, facts when they are once fairly established, react upon our lives. But the words are often perverted to yet darker meanings—suggesting visions of unpardonable sins, of fruitless agonies of personal repentance,—with which souls under strong conviction not seldom torment themselves, and with which the text has absolutely nothing whatever to do. A man seeking change of heart with an agony of tears, pleading with God to renew him, to restore him, and to cherish him to new life and hope, yet spurned from the gate of mercy, flung forth accursed from the arms of love, is a picture which, blessed be God, has no original in the Divine word. No! thus runs the gospel: "*Come unto me, all ye that labour and are heavy laden, and I will give you rest. Take my yoke upon you, and learn of me; for I am meek and lowly in heart, and ye shall find rest unto your souls. For my yoke is easy, and my burden is light.*" "*Ask, and it shall be given you; seek, and ye shall find; knock, and it shall be opened unto you.*" "*For every one that asketh receiveth, and he that seeketh findeth; and to him that knocketh it shall be opened.*" "*If ye, being evil, know how to give good gifts unto your children, how much more shall your Father which is in heaven give the Holy Spirit to them that ask him?*" "*Whoso cometh unto me I will in no wise cast him out.*" "*This man, because he continueth ever, hath an unchangeable priesthood; wherefore he is able also to save them to the uttermost that come unto God by him, seeing he ever liveth to make intercession for them.*"

If any who reads these words has ever made this text a stumbling-block, has ever suffered the devil to thrust the thought into his heart that he has sinned too deeply for repentance, and wandered too far for return—that he can but lie moaning and weeping like Esau, and pleading with anguished heart for repentance, to find his moans rained back in anathemas, and his tears with the fire of the wrath of the Lamb,—let him sweep back the thought as an unholy thing to the devil who inspired it, and cling to the outstretched hand of Him who "*will not break the bruised reed, who will not quench the smoking flax, but will bring forth judgmedt unto truth.*"

The text has literally nothing to do with personal repentance before God. No man can spiritually seek a place of repentance carefully with tears, and fail to find it, for the very act is an act of repentance. I do not care to discuss the question whether the repentance here spoken of is a change in the mind of Isaac, or of Esau himself. In either case the meaning is substantially the same. He found no means of reversing the decree, of winning the blessing of the firstborn, of inducing his father to recall the benediction which had been treacherously diverted to the younger, though he sought it carefully with tears. If it were possible that this text, in all its dreadful meaning, could bear on personal repentance for sin, and frighten men from it lest after all it should be hopeless, it would deny the fundamental ideas and promises of the gospel; nay, it would itself "*trample under foot the Son of God, and count the blood of the covenant wherewith he was sanctified an unholy thing, and do despite to the Spirit of grace.*"

No! the text is a very solemn and even terrible warning of the irrevocable character of deeds done in folly or frenzy; the inexorable character of the fate which takes possession of them when once they have gone forth from us, and which makes by them, it may be in spite of our tears and prayers and desperate struggles, a complete revolution in our lives.

Esau's history is but the repetition of the history of the fall. And it is a history which we all constantly repeat in the critical moments of our lives. Esau fell as Adam fell, and fundamentally for the same reason. Adam despised his birthright, and thought that there was a readier way to the satisfaction of the desires of his heart. Esau by one act changed, not his own history and destiny only, but the destiny of a great nation; Adam changed, by his one sin, the destiny of a great world. "*Wherefore,*" says the apostle, "*as by one man sin entered into the world, and death by sin, and so death passed upon all men.*" (Rom. v. 12.) Adam, like Esau, saw through the eyes of Eve that the "*tree was good for food, and that it was pleasant to the eyes, and a tree to be desired to make one wise.*" What good shall my birthright do to me, he said practically when he saw the forbidden fruit, and he sold it; and that moment's work for him, for you, for me, for all the myriad human generations, can never be recalled in time or in eternity. There is something very much nobler here than in Esau's profaneness. It was not in a moment of sensual lust that our first father sold his own birthright and ours. The desire of wisdom, or what he took for wisdom, had much to do with the force of the temptation; but the essence of the matter is the same: Adam and Esau both chose, in the place of the good which God had provided for them, a good which they provided for themselves. Bitterly Adam, like Esau, repented of his folly, and sought to undo his work. When the wilderness lay cold and bare before him, and the flaming sword of the cherubim guarded the backward path to the bright abodes which he had lost for ever, he measured for the first time the full significance of his transgression. And when the sun set angry and lurid on the wilderness, and the moaning winds swept hoarsely over the waste, while a shudder shook the breast of nature as the tempest clouds gathered in the sullen sky, Adam caught the infection of the tremor, and watched with quivering eye the awful conflict of the forces which had broken loose from his allegiance, and which seemed to come thundering on as the doomsmen of the death which his Judge had decreed. Think you that then his heart did not cling to the memories of the splendours and serenities of Eden with passionate longing; think you that he did not prostrate himself in an agony of frenzied supplication that the barred portal might be unclosed again, that the fiery sword might be sheathed, that the flowers of Eden might again spring beneath his footsteps, while the balmy breezes whispered a blessing as they played around the field of his labour and his bower of rest?

And what has been the long and bitter cry of man's sad history? O God, reverse the sentence, reopen the gate of paradise, revoke the curse, let the sunlight of

Eden shine once more on a holy, peaceful, and happy world! This is the great burden of human literature in all its deeper and more sacred utterances; it is the meaning of all the world's great poems, the refrain of all its immortal hymns. Recall the curse! let life again become pure, peaceful, and blessed! Men, nations, ages have agonized over the sentence; but they have found no place of repentance, no means to change the mind of the Judge or their own condition as the subjects of it, though they have sought it carefully with tears. Esau was the rejected of the birthright; you and I are the rejected of Eden. Sinners we are by nature and proclivity, with a sinner's burdens, a sinner's experience, and a sinner's doom. And there is no way to change the past, to rid us of the burden, to cancel the sentence, to mitigate the anguish of a life on which the devil has seared the shameful brand; no way to force the barred gates of paradise, even by the banded energies of a pain-racked, sin-tormented world.

And I suppose that the private experience of most men furnishes the key to this. Who has not known something of the agony with which one dark deed of passion, lust, falsehood, knavery, baseness, can torture a human heart? Look back. Is there nothing in the past, rising up at this moment in the full menace of its hateful form, clear as the ghost of Banquo before his murderer's sight, which you would give your wealth, nay, some of you would give worlds if they had them, to undo; if conscience might but recover its serenity, and life its brightness; if the leprous flesh of their experience might again become, like Naaman's, fair, pure, and sweet as the flesh of a little child. It is not every Gehazi whose leprosy comes out in his flesh, and makes him loathsome to his fellows. How many Gehazis move about among us, burying their leprosy within, but none the less plague-stricken and perilous! Happy those who have no dark chambers in their being, haunted by the skeletons of their dead lusts, sins, or crimes—skeletons which never fail to come forth at their banquets to scare them, choosing ruthlessly the hours of their festivity and triumph to murder all their joys. There may be some readers of these words who know this in all its horror, in whom the anguish of the irrevocable and irreparable has killed all the joy of life—a word spoken, a passion indulged, a deed done, which in one brief moment has drawn a brooding shadow over the once sunlit landscape of their lives. And you have wept and prayed, lying prostrate on the cold ground, beseeching the merciful God that He would blot out the record from your memory and from the lives which it has embittered and cursed; but "the heaven has been as brass, the earth beneath has been as iron." The word "irrevocable" has forced its meaning upon you in all its terrible sternness, and you have needed no commentary to expound, or preacher to drive home, the meaning of the sentence, "*Beware lest there be any fornicator, or profane person, as Esau, who for one morsel of meat sold his birthright. For ye know how that afterward, when he would have inherited the blessing, he was rejected: for he found no place of repentance, though he sought it carefully with tears.*"

And if there may be some readers who know this experience in all its horror, there are a multitude who know it in its more modified forms, and who find it terrible enough even then. Who has not had forced upon him the misery of regrets or remorse, the causes of which remain unalterable, fixed as the stars in their orbits, and the fruits of which leave deep traces on the experience and the destiny through time, yes, and through eternity? Did David, think you, ever look coldly or carelessly on his bold soldier's bloody grave? Was there no sad shadow, to his eye, around the beauty of Bathsheba's child, which no murmured "Jedidiah" could chase away? Was his home ever free from the shadow, from the hour when Nathan's "Thou art the man" drove conviction home, and wrung from him the most bitter cry of a sinner's anguish which has found record in the literature of our world? Few things in the book of history are more terrible than the sorrow which entered David's home, the discord which rent his kingdom, the anguish which pierced his heart, from the hour of his great transgression. A sad, care-worn, broken man, he finished his course and went down to his grave. Compare the David of 1 Kings i., ii., with the young shepherd in his early prime, if you would estimate the havoc which one great sin may make in a noble life. Ah! in a measure we all know it, in some form or other; words, deeds, outbursts of passion, which have wrung dear hearts with anguish, sundered precious bonds of love, have sullied reputation, clouded prospects, withered hopes, or blighted the promise of lives which we were bound to cherish, or of our own. And we would give worlds to blot out their record, and to repair the evil which has been wrought; but it remains engraven with an iron pen in the rock for ever: man cannot obliterate it, and God will not.

To complete the subject, let me ask you to consider two thoughts.

1. These dread seasons of crucial trial, on which the future of life, nay of eternity, is hanging, never come upon us in a moment.

It would appear from the text that one morsel of meat settled the question of the birthright; that one hard, hot morning's chase settled the destinies of peoples for all time. That is one side of it, the outside. But the real settlement of the question was made already; any trifle will serve to disclose what has already established itself as the permanent character within. Esau had nursed his contempt for the birthright by a thousand daily lustings and cravings; many a bitter scoff too he had flung at Jacob's pious and meditative mood. Things like this never stand alone. The life of the chosen family is described in words of wonderful beauty and power in Heb. xi. 8–14. "*By faith Abraham, when he was called to go out into a place which he should after receive for an inheritance, obeyed; and he went out, not knowing whither he went. By faith he sojourned in the land of promise, as in a strange country, dwelling in tabernacles with Isaac and Jacob, the heirs with him of the same promise. For he looked for a city which hath foundations, whose builder and maker is God. Through faith also Sara herself received strength to conceive seed, and was delivered of a child when she was past age, because she judged him faithful who had promised. Therefore sprang there even of one, and him as good as dead, so many as the stars of the sky in multitude, and as the sand which is by the sea shore innumerable. These all died in faith, not having received the promises, but having seen them afar off, and were persuaded of them, and embraced them, and confessed that they were strangers and pilgrims on the earth. For they that say such things declare plainly that they seek a country."* This life Jacob believed in profoundly; this life Esau as profoundly despised. He despised it all, and made his contempt abundantly apparent. "*And Esau was forty years old when he took to wife Judith the daughter of Beeri the Hittite, and Bashemath the daughter of Elon the Hittite. Which were a grief of mind unto Isaac and to Rebekah*" (Gen. xxvi. 34, 35). This shows how thoroughly out of sympathy with the spirit of the chosen race he was from the first, and remained through life. All his sympathies and associations were with the pagans around him. Jacob was the true heir of the promise, for he believed in it; Esau its outcast, for he despised it, and had despised it from the first. His every act had expressed his contempt of it, and the sale of the birthright for a mess of pottage but completed the witness that he was a profane person, a pagan at heart. These moments mark the crises for which a long train of thought and habit has prepared. Many a secret sin, born of luxury and nursed by royal power and splendour, broke out into the daylight when David looked upon Bathsheba, and filled his life with unutterable sorrow and shame. God takes no man in a hasty moment and brands him reprobate. A thousand daily touches through long years have shaped the image which there reveals itself, and

G 2

on which is moulded the everlasting destiny. The little sins of life are busily, hour by hour, creating the great sins. The small habits and actions, which we allow to pass unrebuked—they seem to be such trifles—soon pass away beyond the power of memory to recall; but they leave their ineffaceable trace on our constitution and character, and lay silently the train of some great outburst of lust, passion, or wickedness, like Esau's or David's. Then is written a record on our nature and destiny which one day we shall agonize to blot out; but the inexorable eye looks coldly down on the frenzied pleader, and the stony lips fashion themselves into a voiceless "Too late!" Meet sin, meet all the devil's seductions and enticements, sternly on the threshold, and the citadel remains for ever sure.

2. The irrevocable is not the irreparable, through the abounding mercy and grace of God.

Things cannot be obliterated or abolished. They remain, and their record remains, for ever. But, blessed be God, they may be transmuted, and wear Divine forms of beauty and joy. And this is what redemption means. Eden is closed for ever. To abolish the condition of man as a sinner, otherwise than by one grand sentence of doom which would abolish his existence as a creature, is beyond the power even of heaven. A sinner's lot you inherit, a sinner's experience you must know, a sinner's agony you must taste, a sinner's horror of darkness you must pass through—to the pit, if the birthright never again seems to you beautiful and glorious, a thing to be won by toil and tears and prayers; but if your soul pines in its rioting, if it sickens in its worldly wealth and splendour, if the question forces itself upon you as it never seems to have forced itself upon Esau, "*What shall it profit a man if he gain the whole world and lose his own soul, or what shall a man give in exchange for his soul?*" then the sinner's anguish, from which there is no escape for any one of us, may be made by Christ's dear love the strait gate to the splendour, the glory, the bliss of heaven. And this is Redemption. Divine love, love that could die, love that *did* die, that its beloved ones might not die, is the solvent which transmutes all the shame and pain of sin to heavenly glory and bliss. "*Where sin abounded, grace did much more abound; that as sin had reigned unto death, even so might grace reign through righteousness, unto eternal life, by Jesus Christ our Lord.*" Here is no reversal, no obliteration of the past, mark you; the thing that was is and shall be; no power in the universe can blot out its trace. The experience of a sinner is part of your being, and in its transmuted form must remain part of your being, through eternity. These wounds and sores of sin, suffused by Christ's great love, become the lustrous pearls of heaven. Nothing in the past, I care not how dark or damning it may be, is irreparable by the love which "*endured the cross and despised the shame,*" that it might win the right and the power to redeem. There is no sin whose stains may not be wept out at the Redeemer's feet. There is no life which may not win "She hath loved much, for she hath much forgiven" as its record, earnest of a rapture of eternal bliss. But dream not that the path can be an easy one, and that penitence can transmute the sorrow into joy by a word. You have done that whose issues could only be undone by the agony and bloody sweat of Gethsemane, the cross and passion of Calvary; and you too must die, die to sin, that you may live to God. The flesh, which has despised your birthright, must be mortified, crucified, by grace. "*I am crucified with Christ*" you must learn to say; you must know the fellowship of the sufferings of your Master, and taste the cup of which He drank the dregs, or the lost birthright is lost for ever, and the deed done on earth remains irreparable as well as irrevocable through eternity.

VII.

THE CURSE OF THE GROUND.

"Cursed is the ground for thy sake."—GEN. iii. 17.

ARE these words part of a curse, or part of a blessing? Are they a sentence on man, the doom of his transgression, or the first stage of a process destined to issue in the redemption of the heir of promise from sorrow and sin for ever? Few phrases are more frequently on our lips than "the curse of labour." Men, women, yea little children, overburdened and crushed by the stern toil which is the necessity of their existence, easily catch up the sentence, and submit to the necessity in the sullen bitter mood with which a slave accepts his chastisement, or a criminal the sentence of doom. Few things are more firmly fixed in our minds than that the toil and the strain of life are God's curse on transgression, having merciful bearings and issues no doubt for the man who lovingly submits to the discipline, but in themselves evil and hateful, born of sin, and a part of death.

I propose to examine this idea in the present discourse, and to endeavour to estimate this curse upon the ground in its bearings on man's development as a spiritual being, and his relations to his Redeemer, God. That toil, care, and pain spring out of the one great act of transgression which every life repeats is the plain and indisputable affirmation of the word of God. The dark tones of man's present life gloom against a background of radiant brightness and beauty; in the childhood of humanity, as in the life of every human child, Eden shines behind all the toil and sorrow of the world. There has been a grand cataclysm in man and in nature. The structure of the world has been rent and contorted, and the fractures and contortions repeat themselves in life. "*Sin entered into the world, and death by sin;*" "*God made man upright, but he sought out many inventions,*" are the sentences of a sound philosophy, estimating the facts of consciousness and history, as well as statements of the word of God. There has been a fall, a rupture, by the sinful guilty action of the freewill of the creature, of the pristine perfect relation between man and God and man and the world. Transgression, the sinful exercise of freedom, is the fundamental fact of man's present nature and life; and the sentence on the transgressor, the inevitable sentence, "*the soul that sinneth it shall die,*" lies at the root of all the bitter anguish of the world.

There are abundant signs of the action of terribly destructive and desolating forces in the physical structure of the world. The earth has been torn and convulsed as by the spasm of some great agony, and the signs of it lie thick around. Huge beds of rock, thousands of feet in thickness, have been cracked and shivered like potsherds; streams of molten metal have been injected into the fissures, and have surged through the rents and swept vast floods of burning lava over the smiling plains. There must have been times in the history of the development of this earth, fair and calm as it lies now under the sun, when its whole structure must have been shaken to the very centre; when there was dread peril lest, like some lost planet, it should be shattered into fragments and fill its orbit with a cloud of wreck. But some sure hand has helped earth's travail, and has brought forth out of the chaos of struggle and storm an orderly, smiling, serene, and beautiful world. The signs of past agony are there, to those whose eye can pierce the surface; but a loving hand has clothed it all with a glow of beauty and a robe of grace. The regions where the convulsion was fiercest, where the scars are deepest, are the regions of glorious mountain beauty, whither pilgrims wend as to nature's most sacred shrine. The rents and chasms, clothed with the most splendid forests, with streams leaping and sparkling through the emerald meadows to the hollows below, breathe nothing but beauty, and stir all hearts to joy and praise. The touch of the destroyer is everywhere masked by beauty; and out of the chaos of confusion God has drawn forth, what never could have been but for the chaos, the infinite variety, the grace, the splendour, the glory of the world.

This mystery of order and beauty, of cosmos, which reveals itself to us in nature, unveils itself too in man's spiritual world. Life, the life of the human, bears traces everywhere of kindred dislocation. A great convulsion has rent man's nature, has torn it away from God and from Eden, and scattered what, but for a redeeming restoring hand, would have been blasted wrecks, about the world. Toil, pain, care, anguish have chased the serenity and bliss of paradise from man's heart and from man's world. Earth is full of wailing, and life of misery. Looking at its surface aspects, we are tempted to call this life of man the abortion of freedom, and to cry with Job, with Jeremiah, Why did it not perish before it saw the sun? Look deeper. As in nature, so in man's life, a loving restoring hand has been working; the wastes of sin are already clothed with some tints of greenness; flowers of rare beauty and splendour spring up on what sin had made a dreary, blasted desert. The moral chaos, touched by the hand of the Divine love, the love of God the Redeemer, already puts on some dress of beauty; nay, it glows here and there with a nascent glory whose fountain is beyond the stars. Some vision of a grand and glorious purpose of redemption unveils itself as we search the secrets of man's sad history. "*Where sin abounded,*" we read in the book of life as well as in the book of Scripture, "*grace did much more abound: That as sin hath reigned unto death, even so might grace reign, through righteousness unto eternal life, by Jesus Christ our*

Lord." (Rom. v. 20, 21.) What we see accomplished helps us to realize the visions of the prophetic word. "*The wilderness and the solitary place, shall be glad for them; and the desert shall rejoice, and blossom as the rose. It shall blossom abundantly, and rejoice even with joy and singing: the glory of Lebanon shall be given unto it, the excellency of Carmel and Sharon; they shall see the glory of the Lord, and the excellency of our God.*" "*Then the eyes of the blind shall be opened, and the ears of the deaf shall be unstopped. Then shall the lame man leap as an hart, and the tongue of the dumb sing: for in the wilderness shall waters break out, and streams in the desert. And the parched ground shall become a pool, and the thirsty land springs of water: in the habitation of dragons where each lay, shall be grass with reeds and rushes. And an highway shall be there, and a way, and it shall be called The way of holiness: the unclean shall not pass over it; but it shall be for those: the wayfaring men, though fools, shall not err therein. No lion shall be there, nor any ravenous beast shall go up thereon, it shall not be found there; but the redeemed shall walk there. And the ransomed of the Lord shall return and come to Zion with songs, and everlasting joy upon their heads: they shall obtain joy and gladness, and sorrow and sighing shall flee away.*" (Isa. xxxv. 1, 2, 5–10.) Sin, the sin of the first parent, which every child of Adam repeats, is the fundamental fact of man's being; no religion, no philosophy, which makes light of it can lay firm hold of man's conscience and heart. But, blessed be God, grace is the crowning fact; and it is the crown which will remain conspicuous through eternity.

The sentence on sin then is a dread reality. "*The soul that sinneth it shall die*" remains as God's judgment record, which no art or effort of man can cancel. But in this first sentence on His sinful child God has wondrously interwoven benediction and judgment, warning and promise, words of life and dooms of death. On the serpent the curse is decisive and final: "*And the Lord*

God said unto the serpent, Because thou hast done this, thou art cursed above all cattle, and above every beast of the field; upon thy belly shalt thou go, and dust shalt thou eat all the days of thy life." (Gen. iii. 14.) But the sternness relaxes and the doom melts into a promise, when the Judge addresses Himself to man. The very curse on the serpent is pregnant with blessing to the woman and her seed; the Executor of the Lord's judgment on the tempter is the everlasting triumphant Redeemer of mankind. And throughout the sentence on our race blessing ranges in fellowship with judgment; and the sternest words, prophets of many ills and sorrows, are rich benedictions in disguise. And this "*cursed is the ground*" is amongst them. It sounds hard and stern, and prophesies a long and hard apprenticeship of toil and pain; but stern as it seems, it is part of the blessing and not of the cursing, of the benediction and not of the doom. It describes the first stage of the redemptive process of which the sentence on the serpent had spoken, and is the condition of man's elevation out of the estate of a sinful, suffering, degraded creature to the friendship, fellowship, and likeness of God. In order that we may appreciate this, and see the true meaning and bearing of the judgment, I shall ask you to consider with me—

I. The range of the sentence.

II. Its work.

I. The range of the sentence. It is the sentence, as far as it bears on man's present condition and experience, that I wish to consider,—the "men must work and women must weep" aspect of our life—excluding the deeper and more tremendous question of death and its issues. Not that any full consideration of the one is possible without reference to the other. The whole sentence hangs together; our life is of one texture, one warp runs through the whole piece; and every groan, every pain, every bead of sweat upon the brow, every shadow that glooms over the life, has its full interpretation in the fact that "*sin has entered into the world, and death by sin;*" all pain is truly a beginning to die. But for our present purpose it is possible sufficiently to isolate the conditions of man's life as the workman and the sufferer, and to consider how they bear, benignly or malignly, on his essential interests as a spiritual being and his education for the destiny which through grace sin has been instrumental to create rather than to destroy. The elements of the sentence which are closely connected with the cursing of the ground, which in fact are links of the same chain, are three:—

Toil—pain—care.

1. Toil. This is fundamental. On this man's existence hangs; to pause here is to stop the pulse of life. "*And unto Adam he said, Because thou hast hearkened unto the voice of thy wife, and hast eaten of the tree of which I commanded thee, saying, Thou shalt not eat of it: cursed is the ground for thy sake; in sorrow shalt thou eat of it all the days of thy life; Thorns also and thistles shall it bring forth to thee; and thou shalt eat the herb of the field: In the sweat of thy face shalt thou eat bread, till thou return unto the ground; for out of it wast thou taken: for dust thou art, and unto dust shalt thou return.*" (Gen. iii. 17–19.) The life of man in Eden was as free from toil as the life of a bee among the limes. Toil is wearing, wasting work; work to which no inward impulse, but the pressure of a stern necessity, moves us; work which we must do, whether we love it or whether we hate it, whether it gently tasks us or strains and exhausts our wearied powers; work which compels us to put aside much that we would infinitely more gladly work at, which cuts us off from pleasant occupation, profitable to our intellectual and social life; work, in a word, which puts a yoke upon us, a yoke which wears and galls; work which makes us moan, and curse the day that we were born to it, and fills us with wild, rebellious passion, which vents itself in railings, blaspheming the wisdom and goodness of the Creator and the

divine order and beauty of the world. This is the work which we sinners are born to; work which urges us with bloody spur, and exacts a tribute of our life-blood as it drives us through the merciless round. This is toil. This is what the curse of the ground has done for us; we eat our bread, not joyously, thankfully, as in Eden, but in the sweat of brow, brain, and heart. How bright the contrast of the Eden life! "*And the Lord God planted a garden eastward in Eden; and there he put the man whom he had formed. And out of the ground made the Lord God to grow every tree that is pleasant to the sight, and good for food; the tree of life also in the midst of the garden, and the tree of knowledge of good and evil. And a river went out of Eden to water the garden; and from thence it was parted, and became into four heads. . . . And the Lord God took the man, and put him into the garden of Eden, to dress it and to keep it.*" (Gen. ii. 8–10, 15.) Sweet, light labour, parent of yet sweeter rest. To dress and to keep the garden! A garden planted by the hand of the Lord. The fairest, brightest garden of the creation; dewy fragrance, radiant colour, splendid form; all that imagination can dream of beauty and glory, bathing man's life in an atmosphere of ravishing, exquisite, inexhaustible joy. One act of transgression, and the garden vanished. Like a dream it faded; and hard, stern realities, unlovely hues, ungraceful forms, unkindly elements, rose round Adam in its room. Instead of the garden where the touch of the Divine hand still lingered in forms and tones of bewildering beauty, a bare hard wilderness stretched everywhere around him, whence not a morsel of bread could be wrung but by the most strenuous labour; where not a gleam of beauty, not a nestling nook of verdure, would smile on him, until he had created it by earnest, persistent, and wasting toil. "*Cursed is the ground.*"

2. Pain. Part of the sentence of toil is pain. "*Unto the woman he said, I will greatly multiply thy sorrow, and thy conception; in sorrow thou shalt bring forth children;*

and thy desire shall be to thy husband, and he shall rule over thee." (Gen. iii. 16.) The fountain-head of pain is travail. It begins at birth, it ends in death; life on the whole, between the limits, is one long struggle to endure. "Men must work, and women must weep." It is not a complete division: for men weep while they work, and women work while they weep; toil and tears are the bitter heritage of us all. But the man has on the whole the chief share of the strain, the woman of the pain, of life. Her life, if she has a woman's nobleness and the sense of a woman's mission, is one long travail. This bearing and rearing of children is symbolic. What is the life of all noble, unselfish, ministering natures, but the continual bringing forth, with sore pain of travail, of things which shall gladden and enrich the world? But pain is a great mystery. Why the good God, serenely blessed, should suffer pain to torment His child! How the heavenly powers can bear to look upon it, to hear all the moans of anguish, to see all the wrestlings of pain which each moment distract and waste the beings whom they love! For much of the pain of life man himself is, directly and in the first instance, responsible. He makes it, in spite of God, by his insane folly, passion, or lust. But how much lies at the door of the heavenly Ruler, is His word, His ordinance, the discipline which He presses sternly on His child! Pain, that torments and maddens him while he works; pain that pierces him from everything that he touches, everything that he delights in, every being that he loves; pain, that searches the roots of his courage and endurance, which makes the marrow quiver in his bones, the blood curdle in his heart; pain, which rings from a man who is the very type of endurance the most bitter curses, the most fierce anathemas on the very sunlight which shines on him, on birth and all its agony, on life and all its intolerable woe. "*In sorrow shalt thou bring forth children,*" and everything which is freighted with any portion of thy life. Pain in birth; tears in the eyes of helpless infants on their mother's bosom; the paths of the wilderness wet with the tears of brave men and women wrestling with pain too sharp for endurance; tears rung out from the glazing eye, when it settles for one painless moment into the fixed, cold stare of death!

3. Care. "*Dust thou art.*" Here lies the secret of care. I believe that these words suggest altogether the most bitter and miserable experience of mankind. Toil may be borne, pain may be borne; but who in his own strength can wrestle with and master care? Man's condition is that of the most dependent of beings, while the things which he needs for the satisfaction of his nature refuse to recognise the mastery of his hand. He comes into the world the most helpless of all the infants of creation. It is horrible to imagine what a human infant, in the hands of a careless or cruel parent, may be made to endure. And this condition of his infancy follows him through life: he is really an infant, a nursling, as dependent for the daily bread of body, mind, and spirit on supplies which he cannot command, as an infant at the mother's breast. So large is the range of his necessities, so infinite his wants, that he needs just the arm and the treasure of the Omnipotent to supply it. And the sentence "*dust thou art*" meets him everywhere. He feels it in the miserable infirmity of his arm; he reads it in the accidents of life and the decrees of fate. He knows that there are things needful to his happiness, needful to his very life, things which he would die rather than miss; and yet they mock the puny efforts of his arm, the feeble breath of his prayer. He sees them passing hopelessly beyond the limits of his horizon, and he must live on and drag on from day to day, a broken, wretched, beggared life. Who has not groaned in utter misery over his wretched helplessness in the hand of calamity, as though his life were the sport of a demon, and all his pleasant things but instruments of torture, with which some malignant spirit can torment his soul and desolate his life? He is in the presence of masses and forces in

the creation, which oppress and crush his spirit; but there seems to him a maligner demon behind the veil of the creation, who delights to make sport of his weakness and burn in the sentence "*dust thou art*" upon the tablets of his heart. Toil, pain, care, these are the bitter ingredients of his experience; these make up how much of the daily course and order of his life. Verily men may well imagine that a curse was meant here rather than a blessing, and dream that a devil, a malignant spirit, is nearer to them and more potent on their lives than God. So dread is the pressure, that in the absence of revelation, in the absence of the assurance "*Like as a father pitieth his children, so the Lord pitieth them that fear Him, for He knoweth their frame, He remembereth that they are dust,*" devil worship becomes inevitably the religion of the pagan world.

Such is the range of the sentence. Now let us ask—

II. What is its work? Is it malign or benignant? Is it, in its very essence, a curse or a blessing to man?

Our first notion on reading these words, "*Cursed is the ground for thy sake,*" is naturally that part of the curse on man has fallen on the ground. It is cursed "*for thy sake,*" by transition of the curse from thee. But the word bears a nobler meaning. "For thy sake" may as well, nay better, mean "with a view to thy good." The root of the sentence would still be transgression. There had been no need of toil, care, and pain, had not sin entered into the world. But sin having entered, toil, care, and pain are ordained for the sake of man in the loftiest sense; they are the most perfect ordinance which could be framed to bless him (or rather with a view to his full and perfect blessing, for they only begin what higher influence must complete), by the Almighty Father's wisdom, power, and love. I am very anxious that the full force of this statement should be understood. It is quite possible to take the following view of it:—Man having placed himself before God in the attitude of a sinner, justice demanded that he should be sentenced: toil, care, pain, and death *are* the sentence, the expression of God's anger against the transgressor, making man the outcast of His love; that then, in pity, God took compassion on the outcast, and began a remedial work, which, while leaving him still for the present under the action of the sentence, sought to rescue him ultimately from its final doom. This would appear to me a very imperfect and partial statement of the truth. To me it seems as if the whole sentence were the expression of the tenderness which began to work in the Father's heart in the very moment of the transgression. The death which is the righteous doom, the inevitable fruit, of sin, is in the very moment of the sentence held in suspense as it were by the promise; and the toil, care, and pain which are expressed in the sentence are the very first steps of the remedial work. The sinner in the very moment of transgression is drawn to the bosom of God's mercy. Since the first promise was spoken, the death which was the sinner's doom can only be tasted in its bitterness by the man who treats the promise as a thing of nought. And all the hard and stern conditions of man's present lot, instead of being the doom of a judgment from which mercy is moved to rescue him, are themselves the motions of mercy by which the work of rescue is begun. This is the principle on which alone it appears to me that the text can be understood.

I do not propose to occupy your thoughts with any of what I may call the minor mercies of the sentence, and the minor ministries of toil, care, and pain to the true development of man. The sentence of toil at once began man's higher education. It brought him firmly and sternly, but not malignly, into contact with the laws which he had broken, and whose penalties he had defied. Not a morsel of bread could he win without again submitting to them; humbly, absolutely, utterly, he must become their servant if he would win the lightest blessing from their hand. But the blessing was there, it was clearly possible that he should win it. Hard and stern as has been his toil, through all these ages it has nourished him. Nature, though stern, is the reverse of malignant; all her conditions are not penal, but disciplinary; the sentence placed him at the foot of the ladder, a vision of which Jacob once saw, whose highest rungs are lost in heaven. But instead of tracing this, I wish to dwell rather on the ministry of the sentence at once and directly to the unfolding of man's Divinest life. The more you look at it, the more clearly I think will it become apparent to you that it is through toil, and care, and pain alone that such a being as man can rise to the full height of his godlike stature, and grow into the likeness and the fellowship of God. Let me ask you then to consider these three points:—

1. Through toil, and care, and pain, man becomes a creator—not a servant, but a master workman, and springs, as compared with his condition in Eden, into a higher region of life.

2. Through toil, and care, and pain, he becomes acquainted with all the experience of a father; the deepest and noblest relationships unfold their significance, and unutterably enrich and exalt his life.

3. By toil, and care, and pain, he rises to the full and sympathetic knowledge of God his Redeemer, and enters into the holiest fellowship of the universe for ever.

1. The experience which grows out of the sentence constitutes him a creator, a master workman, and lifts him into a higher region of life.

Man in Eden was the loyal, loving servant of his Creator, no more. God "*placed him in the garden to dress and to keep it.*" Fair, sweet, genial work, like life in one of the soft bright islands of the Pacific. Every moment an exquisite sensation, every movement a pulse of joy. Well! there you have the whole of it. And I say boldly there is not enough of it. To dress and to keep even a paradise is poor, slight work for a being framed and endowed like man. It was inevitable that sooner or later he should get to the end of its interest and the lees of its joy. A strong, hardy, brave, cultivated Englishman soon gets to the end of the soft, sweet life of the Pacific island. It suits the islanders, who are mostly pulp, morally and mentally,—the human jelly-fish, without muscle and fibre; but there is not enough of it for the cultivated and developed man. Toil, pain, and care set the exile of Eden at once about higher work. He went forth with a great sorrow in his heart, and a great shadow over his life, into the hard stern wilderness. There he had not to *dress and to keep* a garden, but to make one, and that is altogether higher and nobler work. A higher range of faculties was at once called into action. He had to create fruitful fields and homesteads, and to frame a new paradise in imagination, which his strenuous toil, pain, and care were to realize in time. His creative work as a husbandman is symbolic of all his creation, his work as parent, thinker, artist, poet, and master of the world. In Eden everything was made for him, and was ready to his hand; in the world he had to make, or at any rate to mould, everything, and to make his hand ready for an infinite variety of work. And what does this constructive creative toil imply? It means that he had to discover, to think out, and to reproduce, by the utmost strain his faculties would bear, the thoughts of God. He had to study nature, and to master her methods; he had to discover the uses of his powers and the possibilities of his life. He rose at once sad and stricken, but grand through the gentleness which had made him great, to the fulness of a godlike stature; and what are toil, and pain, and care, through life's brief day, if they lift man up to this excellent glory of his manhood, the power to think, to work, to create, in the track and after the method of God?

2. By toil, and pain, and care, man becomes acquainted with the experience of a father; the deepest and noblest relationships unfold to him their significance, and unutterably enrich and exalt his life.

Travail is the symbolic pain. "*In sorrow shalt thou*

bring forth children;" and in sorrow all the products of the higher life are born. The question is very simple. Ask a woman, when the cry of her first-born sounds in her ear, and its cheek nestles on her breast, how far the joy transcends the pain. She can only murmur—"Unspeakably," and clasp her nursling closer to her heart. How much the pain enters into and exalts the joy, who shall tell? Ask the man, a man like poor Palissy, or the blind bard who got £10 for a "Paradise Lost," how the account stands with him. He can but answer, The work, mighty as has been its cost, is the joy and glory of my life—perhaps because of its very cost. In a grand and glorious country you must have the mountains and the valleys; the depths measure the heights, you cannot divorce them; the two make the beauty which pilgrims come from far to gaze upon, whose vision quickens the life in its dull springs. And all the toil, and care, and pain which our intimate, our dearest relations with our fellows cost us, as husband, wife, parent, brother, sister, friend, teacher, poet, prophet, will be found closely, essentially connected with our highest, purest, and most enduring joys. Mothers shall be our witnesses: theirs is the typical pain, and care, and toil. How say you, careworn, toiling, but rejoicing mothers? Where lie the springs of your sweetest pleasure, where lie the treasures which you would guard with life? The toils, the cares, the pangs that grow out of our human relations in a sad, struggling, mortal world like this, call forth and string to the finest tension passions, loves, faculties, thoughts, energies, which Eden never could have developed. There was little that was noble in the words of Adam on Eve's temptation in the garden; indeed, on neither side does any nobleness appear. But in the wilderness there are men by myriads who would shield the woman they love from a pang or a reproach, and count the cost light if they gave their lives. Oh! my friends, take a large and noble measure of the breadth of thought, feeling, faculty, which toil, and pain, and care develop; and remember that every filament of love and care which binds you to a human being, though intensely sensitive, and therefore in a world like this inevitably doomed to throb with pain, is a tentacle of your spirit life which can never be detached from it but by your own baseness, and through which life, joy, rapture will flow into it in the world in which sin is beaten, crushed for ever, in which there can be no more tears and no more pain.

One word more.

3. Toil, care, pain raise man to the full and sympathetic knowledge of God his Redeemer, and bring him into the holiest fellowship of the universe for ever.

I say bring him. That is God's purpose; that is what God means by it: but God does not force him. The word must be mixed with faith in them that hear it; faith in the Son of God, who died that the sentence might be a benediction instead of a doom. Some, when they heard, did not, would not believe; and their carcases fell in the wilderness, and their bones whiten the sand.

Toil, care, and pain. Does God know nothing of them? *"He is despised and rejected of men; a man of sorrows, and acquainted with grief: and we hid as it were our faces from him; he was despised, and we esteemed him not. Surely he hath borne our griefs, and carried our sorrows: yet we did esteem him stricken, smitten of God, and afflicted. But he was wounded for our transgressions, he was bruised for our iniquities: the chastisement of our peace was upon him; and with his stripes we are healed. All we, like sheep, have gone astray; we have turned every one to his own way; and the Lord hath laid on him the iniquity of us all. He was oppressed, and he was afflicted; yet he opened not his mouth: he is brought as a lamb to the slaughter, and as a sheep before her shearers is dumb, so he opened not his mouth. He was taken from prison and from judgment: and who shall declare his generation? for he was cut off out of the land of the living: for the transgression of my people was he stricken."* (Isa. liii.

3–8.) Count it the highest ministry of the sentence that it enables you to understand that; count it the highest aim and glory of a man's life to enter into fellowship with that life of the Lord. Hold this to be the deepest, most solemn prayer which has ever been uttered by human lips: "*That I may know him, and the power of his resurrection, and the fellowship of his sufferings: being conformed unto his death; if by any means I may attain unto the resurrection from the dead.*" And grudge no pain, nay glory in every pain, which opens to you a fuller comprehension of the sorrows of the Man of sorrows upon earth, the joy and glory of the Lord of glory in eternity. Light the affliction which is but for a moment: its ministry is unspeakable blessing in this life; you will find it infinite blessing in eternity. Sons of God, wear with joy the marks of sonship! Brethren of Christ, tread with courage in the Brother's footsteps! Heirs of glory, pay gaily with songs the price by which your glory is to be won.

"*What are these which are arrayed in white robes? and whence came they?*" "*These are they which came out of great tribulation, and have washed their robes, and made them white in the blood of the Lamb. Therefore are they before the throne of God, and serve him day and night in his temple; and he that sitteth on the throne shall dwell among them. They shall hunger no more, neither thirst any more; neither shall the sun light on them, nor any heat. For the Lamb which is in the midst of the throne shall feed them, and shall lead them unto living fountains of waters; and God shall wipe away all tears from their eyes.*"

VIII.

THE EASILY BESETTING SIN.

"The sin which doth so easily beset us."—HEB. xii. 1.

THESE words occur at the close of the most brilliant rhetorical passage of the New Testament scripture. They form the point too of the most close, subtle, and profound argument which is to be met with even in the epistles of St. Paul. We constantly use them; no sentence of the Bible is more frequently on our lips. But we isolate them from their surroundings; we handle them as though they dealt with private matters of individual experience, the sins and follies to which each nature in its private propension is specially prone, rather than some broad human fault or infirmity which is the common sin and sorrow of mankind. We must read these words in connection with the great argument of which they form the culmination, and the splendid burst of eloquence which they close; or we shall miss their large and weighty meaning, and shall narrow to a private and partial experience what the writer intends to set forth as the easily besetting sin of mankind. The Epistle to the Hebrews is certainly one of the most important and profound books in the New Testament. Be it by Paul himself, as I believe, or be it by some Pauline man, it is in a measure the keystone of the arch of revelation, if the Apocalypse is its crown. The way in which, in the order of the Divine dispensations, the old grows into the new—the method by which, while so much once ordained by God goes apparently to wreck, to the eye of God and in the judgment of the far-sighted among men nothing Divine really perishes, no Divine promise fails of fulfilment, no Divine purpose or hope misses its fruit—is a subject of supreme importance, the consideration of which is needful to the completeness of Scripture, while it is full of suggestion as a key to the Divine ways, to the successive generations of mankind. Judaism has passed away in every respect in which it is stronger than a memory. It is essentially, though Jews live among us in Christendom by millions, a thing of the past; but the Epistle to the Hebrews, which unfolds the method by which Judaism developed into Christianity, is a living book in our Bibles, as full of vital interest for this present time as it was for the generation which watched with strange awe and wonder the tremendous overthrow of the elect nation, and saw the last fragments of the ritual and order of a Divinely established system swept along by the flood as wreck. There is profound instruction concerning the method of development in Christendom—how the Church grows, and strikes deeper root through the ages, while that which men call the Church and cling to suffers constant shocks, and is ever dropping piecemeal into decay and death—in this sketch of the philosophy of the most remarkable and startling development recorded in man's spiritual history. Whether Paul wrote it or not, it is the work of a man with Paul's grasp of intellect, and saturated with Paul's ideas both of Judaism and Christianity. One can hardly imagine Paul's life-work complete to his own mind without the production of such an essay as this. He alone grasped with perfect clearness the vital relation of the two dispensations; and we can well imagine with what intense earnestness this Hebrew of the Hebrews must have desired to justify his apostolic ministry to his countrymen and to mankind. Be this as it may, and these *a priori* judgments are of little worth in criticism, the book is one of large thoughts, views, and principles, reaching deep down to the foundations on which the edifice of man's spiritual faith and hope is built.

Let us try to realize some of the main difficulties of those to whom it is addressed, whose tormenting doubts and apprehensions it was intended to remove. They would be chiefly, I think, of two kinds; and they might be put into the shape of questions.

1. Can anything which is ordained of God be abrogated?

2. Can the Messiah, the kingly Son of David, be come, while those who follow Him are the world's outcasts, spoiled, persecuted, and slain?

The first is a standing difficulty with all the students of the mysteries of God, in all ages of the world. It pressed on the Hebrew Christians with peculiar force. They and their fathers for ages had believed that a certain visible system had been established on earth by God's own hand, and sustained by His almighty power. It seemed to them as if the very foundations of the universe were shaken, when their temple, their priesthood, their glorious Jerusalem, their beautiful fertile Palestine, vanished like a dream, and left them the beggars and outcasts of mankind.

The second difficulty was equally grave. It touched men where they are ever most sensitive, in their individual experiences and hopes. Can the head of this Christian Church be the God-man, the glorious Being of whom our prophets prophesied, and of whose kingdom they had such brilliant visions, whilst its subjects are despised, hated, and down-trodden, and its princes are the scum and off-scouring of all things unto this day? We say that the Jews were expecting a splendid temporal kingdom, a visible reign of the Messiah in righteousness over a regenerate and exulting world. We say it with a touch of scorn. We may spare our scorn; Christendom is always dreaming of it too. It would be a wonderful thing if the Jews had not nourished some such expectations. All men have not faith. How many Christians understand Christianity better than the Jews understood the Judaism of their times? What is the Papacy but an endeavour to realize this splendid and prosperous reign of Christ, of which Judaism dreamed? A rule of righteousness, peace, and goodwill, under the sceptre of Christ's immediate delegate and regent, is the vision which has haunted in all ages some of the ablest minds in Christendom; and the desire to realize this has been near the heart of some of the most desperate struggles which rent the civilized world throughout the middle age. We cannot wonder at their sad thoughts. We think the same when things much less visibly ordained of God are shattered and swept away as wrecks. The answer of the writer of this epistle to the question which was wrung out of the death agony of that nation and church was substantially this: God does not establish *things*, He plants seeds which grow. The principle of life in the seed is the principle of identity through the successive stages of the development of the organism. The body of man is one, though it changes form very visibly at successive eras, and though every particle of matter composing it is in constant flux, passing away from without, restored by the constructive force of the living principle within. Rise, he says, to a loftier and more comprehensive view of the Divine dispensations. See how the living principle of God's relation to you, to man, as Father and Redeemer, runs through all the dispensations, moulds the outward form of the Church according to the exigencies of the times, and is ever bringing forth new forms as the ages need. See how the germ which was planted before the law grew into the legal dispensation, and how when the leafage and fruitage of that dispensation grew old and withered, as *things* must grow old and perish, the living principle within took new and diviner form, suffered, as all divine things do, death and resurrection, and lived with a new and divine life in a new and regenerated world. "*God, who at sundry times and in divers manners spake in time past unto the fathers by the prophets, hath in these last days spoken unto us by his Son, whom he hath appointed heir of all things, by whom also he made the worlds; who being the brightness of his glory, and the express image of his person, and upholding all things by the word of his power, when he had by himself purged our sins, sat down on the right hand of the Majesty on high; being made so much better than the angels, as he hath by inheritance obtained a more excellent name than they."* (Heb. i. 1–4.)

It ought not to be hard for us to understand and enter into the sore perplexities of the Hebrew believers when they found their ancestral kingdom uprooted, while no sign of the new Messiah's kingdom appeared, except the sway which a shameful cross was wielding over individual human hearts. Can this be the beginning of the kingdom? Can Christ be reigning there, and we His subjects here, the objects of His tenderest care and love, be so harried and tormented for our truth and righteousness as never men have been harried and tormented for lies and sins? Is it credible that God's sons in the world should be the world's outlaws; that those whom the hand of Omnipotence shields should be the helpless victims of the most puny foes? Are slaves and beggars the chief subjects of Messiah's kingdom? Does the fellowship of this new realm draw us into loving, tender communion with the saddest, the poorest, the most ignorant, the most wretched of mankind? Is the life of this new regenerate state a ceaseless struggle, a constant pain, with no issue but by the gate of death, whose apparitors may be a lion's jaws or a headsman's axe? Is the symbol of this splendid empire a cross? The answer to these questions is the text. The question is the sin which so easily besets humanity, you and me quite as intensely as the Hebrews; and the cure for the sin, the answer to the question, is the faith which draws from the writer this splendid eulogy, a faith which scans the bounds of the invisible universe, and measures the range of the Divine thought from the height of the Divine throne. It is as though the writer had said, Looked at on the lower level, by the measures of the things seen and temporal, the lot is dark enough and sad enough: "*If in this life only we have hope in Christ, we are of all men most miserable.*" (1 Cor. xv. 19.) But rise to a higher level. Get up into the mountain, and survey the horizon of a wider world. Search into the nature of man's true well-being, and see where the springs of it rise. Measure the range of man's existence, the endless ages of his being, the boundless faculty of joy or sorrow, of bliss or anguish, that claims eternity as its time. Above all, measure the stature of a man. Study the image after which he is fashioned, the godlike form he wears, the godlike experience he is made to fathom, and the kind of satisfaction which his godlike powers demand, robbed of which they hunger and pine and fill him at last with madness and despair; so shall you comprehend more fully the grandeur and the glory of his Christian vocation—sharing the conflict, the toil, the sorrow, the joy, and the triumph of hisever God. Then lay aside "every weight and the sin that doth so easily beset you." That sin is poverty of faith—a poor-spirited estimate of life, its experiences and its issues; a love for the serfdom of Egypt rather than the freedom of the wilderness, the fleshpots of Goshen rather than the bread of Canaan, the pleasure of the moment rather than the joy which springs from fountains that outlast eternity.

The sin which doth so easily beset us. Want of faith.

I. In ourselves. II. In God. III. In the future.

I. Want of faith in ourselves—poor, base views of our nature, power, and destiny.

The essential dignity of man's nature, as God constituted it, and the utter debasement it has suffered through sin, are facts which in nowise clash or contradict each other. In truth, no man who has not faith enough to comprehend what "*power to become the sons of God*" may mean, as spoken of man, can enter into the depth of anguish and shame wrung out in the confession, "*I was as a beast before thee.*" "*I have heard of thee with the hearing of the ear, but now mine eye seeth thee; wherefore I abhor myself, and repent in dust and ashes.*" At the root of the humiliation, the debasement, lies this want of faith in our higher being and destiny. We prefer the slave's portion, with the slave's security, to the cares and burdens of freedom, with its hopes and joys. The main difficulty in the emancipation of serfs arises always from themselves. They do not care, nay they fear, to be free. The responsibility of self-government and self-control is a burden from which they shrink;—let us creep safely on the lower levels, rather than strain perilously up the mountain paths, with the free air around us, the bright heaven above us, the mists, the clouds, the storms, seething and flashing beneath our feet. This is the cry of our souls—yours and mine. God is ever stirring us to take the higher view of our nature and destiny; we are ever burying ourselves in the lower:—"'*Let us alone, Jesus, thou Son of God.*' Thy words are perilous; they search and judge us; they trouble us in our politics, our pleasures, our trade. We are fairly content as it is; why should we weary ourselves by straining after the higher good, which seems thin, impalpable, and may easily elude our hand? Let us alone; depart out of our coasts." This was the mood of these Hebrew Christians; it is ours. And nothing does the devil's work more surely within us than this feeling that on the whole we were made for poor work, poor interests, and poor joys. Paul seeks to stir us to a nobler mood, to fire something within us which will burn with a heavenly lustre and seek to mingle itself with the brightness of its native skies. Man is made to deal with the substance of things, the eternal substance; you are content to converse with their fleeting shadows. "*For the law, having a shadow of good things to come, and not the very image of the things, can never with those sacrifices which they offered year by year continually make the comers thereunto perfect. For then would they not have ceased to be offered? because that the worshippers once purged should have had no more conscience of sins. But in those sacrifices there is a remembrance again made of sins every year. For it is not pos-*

sible that the blood of bulls and of goats should take away sins." (Heb. x. 1–4.) The heavenly things themselves your minds were made to contemplate, your hearts to love, your spirits to commune with; and you are grovelling amid the ashes of the perishing, while the imperishable, the eternal, passes for ever beyond the range of your sight. Believe in humanity as the first step to a nobler life. Not the poor, weak, trembling humanity which your self-communings reveal to you; but the glorious, Divine humanity which God has set before you to help your infirmity, to recall the memory of the height from which you have fallen, and to kindle the hope of the royal dignity to which you may be restored. Look within; and man seems poor enough, and pitiful enough. But look above: "*We see Jesus who was made a little lower than the angels, for the suffering of death, crowned with glory and honour; that he by the grace of God should taste death for every man.*" Then "*lay aside every weight, and the sin which doth so easily beset you, and run with patience the race that is set before you, looking unto Jesus the author and finisher of our faith; who for the joy that was set before him, endured the cross, despising the shame, and is set down at the right hand of the throne of God.*"

Behold in Him the perfect image of a man, in His life the beauty of a perfect human life. Believe in that image; gaze on it, meditate on it, till contemplation kindles sympathy, and sympathy grows into love. "*Consider the apostle and high-priest of your profession, Christ Jesus*"; and if you tread in His footsteps of present sorrow and humiliation, glory in it, and pray that you may go on to know it more perfectly, "*the power of his resurrection, the fellowship of his sufferings, being made conformable unto his death.*" Believe that all that a man was meant to be, to do, to become, can only grow out of this vital fellowship with Jesus. Believe in Him rather than in the world's ideas, maxims, and hopes. Leave them to the Pagans. You, sons of God, heirs of God, joint-heirs with Christ, learn nobler lessons out of the book of His life, aim at loftier marks, thirst for purer and perennial joys.

II. Poor belief about God—unbelief in the Incarnation, and all its blessed meanings to mankind.

The low and slavish idea of man's character and destiny inevitably infects our views of God and of God's action and purpose in the world. Having poor hope ourselves, we cannot understand God's hope, the hope which lit the path to Calvary, and shed a flood of glorious light around the saddest and most shameful passage of man's sad and painful history. To those who believe that man is the serf of the creation, the Incarnation is incredible. God would be ashamed to be called the God, in any high Christian sense, of such beings as some men believe themselves to be and act as if they were. The Hebrew Christians could not believe in the Incarnation; that is, they were beset with unbelief about it. Their fathers could not believe in their angel guide. A glorious triumphant King, coming to the world in splendour, scattering the hosts of His foes by His thunders, and leading His armies to rapid and easy victory, they could comprehend well enough. But the cross was their stumbling-block. Can the living God suffer shame, anguish, and death, for such beings as we are, for such a kingdom as this Crucified One may be able to win? "*That be far from thee, Lord;*" it is blasphemy to dream of it. They were like a man in poverty and straits, who is always expecting that a splendid fortune will fall to him suddenly, will enable him to make a magnificent figure, and to be a model of dignity, generosity, and manly grace. But the MAN is he who wins his fortune by bearing the strain of toil through long years of patience, and who trains himself by discipline to rule it as a realm when gained. And we are, most of us, of this foolish temper. What wonderful people we should be, we think, if our platform were higher, and a stronger light were thrown upon our lives! If God would but mend our surroundings, our virtue and dignity would appear! Believe that it seemed good to God, that it became God, to reveal to us the truth of this relation between surroundings and life, by sending His Son, in the likeness of sinful flesh, to live the life of God in poverty, sorrow, and shame, and manifest in that depth of humiliation the mystery of the life eternal. "*For it became him, for whom are all things, and by whom are all things, in bringing many sons unto glory, to make the captain of their salvation perfect through sufferings. For both he that sanctifieth and they who are sanctified are all of one: for which cause he is not ashamed to call them brethren, saying, I will declare thy name unto my brethren, in the midst of the church will I sing praise unto thee. And again, I will put my trust in him. And again, Behold I and the children which God hath given me. Forasmuch then as the children are partakers of flesh and blood, he also himself likewise took part of the same; that through death he might destroy him that had the power of death, that is, the devil; aud deliver them who through fear of death were all their lifetime subject to bondage. For verily he took not on him the nature of angels; but he took on him the seed of Abraham. Wherefore in all things it behoved him to be made like unto his brethren, that he might be a merciful and faithful high priest in things pertaining to God, to make reconciliation for the sins of the people. For in that he himself hath suffered being tempted, he is able to succour them that are tempted.*" (Heb. ii. 10–18.)

It was a hard, an incredible saying to many among the Hebrew Christians. In all its deep meaning it is a hard, an incredible saying to us. Do we believe in our heart of hearts that the life of daily denial, cross-bearing, and Divine ministry, missing all earthly honour, golden treasure, and worldly joy, is the life which the Lord God of heaven lived on earth, and glorified earth by living it? Have we an eye for that inner glory? Is that tear-stained path He trod, beautiful, transcendently beautiful, in our sight, as it is to the angels and the white-robed choir on high? Shame on our lives then, if this is the belief of our hearts about it. If we believe that He who was in the form of God, and "*thought it not robbery to be equal with God; but made himself of no reputation, and took upon him the form of a servant and was made in the likeness of men*" (Phil. ii. 6–8), left us an ensample that we should follow in His steps, what are our lives like before Him and before the angels, filled as they are with selfish aims and passions, strivings after things that perish, that crumble to dust as we grasp them; contemptuous as they are of celestial things and powers, of all that made His life luminous to the eye of spirits, of all that He came through shame and anguish to set palpably before the vision of our souls. "*Lay aside the sin that doth so easily beset you*"—this sin of light thoughts of Christ, of the intense reality of His human life, and all the high meanings and inspirations with which it is charged for you, for me, for all mankind. Open wide the gates of your spirit, and let this King of Glory in. "*Lift up your heads, O ye gates; and be ye lift up, ye everlasting doors; and the King of glory shall come in.*" Who is this King of Glory? The Man of Sorrows, He is the King of Glory. Believe, faint heart, and live.

III. Unbelief in the future.

We cannot believe that this is purely a seed-time. Like children, we are for reaping where we have not sown, and gathering where we have not strawed. Or, if by chance we drop a seed into the earth and leave it for a moment, next morning we are digging about it to see if it is growing, and are sick at heart if it promises no immediate fruit. The Hebrew Church demanded the instant fruitage of the death of Christ. "*And Jesus answered them, saying, The hour is come, that the Son of man should be glorified. Verily, verily, I say unto you, Except a corn of wheat fall into the ground and die, it abideth alone; but if it die, it bringeth forth much fruit. He that loveth his life shall lose it; and he that hateth his life in this world shall keep it unto life eternal.*" (John xii. 23–25.) Lord, we have seen the seed corn cast into the ground, we have seen it lie there, we have seen it rise, and where is the harvest? Where is the kingdom? Where are the throngs? Where is the throne? The offence of the cross still lies in the way of triumph. Tribulations are the only gifts of the kingdom still! The writer of this epistle does not care to argue about the moment. Be it so. Be it as bad as you say: tribulations, persecutions, contempt, spoiling of your goods, and bonds. Be it so. "*Ye have not yet resisted unto blood, striving against sin.*" You have not faced the last extremity, and the last extremity may be in store. But what matters? Sons of God, brethren of Christ, citizens of the heavenly state, heirs of everlasting joys and glory, what matters it? "*Behold, the husbandman waiteth for the precious fruit of the earth, and hath long patience for it, until he receive the early and latter rain. Be ye also patient; stablish your hearts: for the coming of the Lord draweth nigh. Grudge not one against another, brethren, lest ye be contemned: behold, the judge standeth before the door. Take, my brethren, the prophets, who have spoken in the name of the Lord, for an example of suffering affliction, and of patience. Behold, we count them happy which endure. Ye have heard of the patience of Job, and have seen the end of the Lord; that the Lord is very pitiful, and of tender mercy.*" (Jas. v. 7–11.) Is patience no longer beautiful, divine, when it is heaven which has to be waited for, a royal sceptre, an everlasting crown? For shame! moaning over the moment's pains, which are the seeds of everlasting joys; over the dust of the husks and shells of the temporal things, when, as they waste and perish, the glorious forms of the things not seen and eternal, which they veiled, appear. I say not, Compare the one with the other, weigh them well, and make your selection. There is no comparison possible. "*I reckon that the sufferings of this present life are not worthy to be compared with the glory that shall be revealed.*" "*For our light affliction, which is but for a moment, worketh for us a far more exceeding and eternal weight of glory; while we look not at the things which are seen, but at the things which are not seen:*

for the things which are seen are temporal; but the things which are not seen are eternal." (2 Cor. iv. 17, 18.) It is blank unbelief to talk about comparison. The one is infinitely small and pitiful; the other is infinitely great, beautiful, and glorious. "*What things were gain to me,*" when the visible things of earth and time filled my sight, "those I have counted loss for Christ. Yea, doubtless, and I count all things but loss, for the excellency of the knowledge of Christ Jesus my Lord: for whom I have suffered the loss of all things, and do count them but dung, that I may win Christ." (Phil. iii. 7, 8.) This is the Christian estimate. This is the true entrenchment of the human spirit against all the floods of calamity which may beat around the rock on which it builds its hopes. Be my lot what it may, my God, my Father ordains it; and He has the power, the will to make every pain, every wound, every heartache, every cross, every shock, the seed of a harvest whose glorious wealth I cannot measure even in my dreams. The power and the will, said I? His strongest promises, His profoundest purposes, are engaged in the fulfilment of the hope which He kindles in my breast, and which makes me master of the world. Nay, He has staked His life, the very existence of His throne, upon it. He has subjected you and me and the vast creation to vanity, "*in hope, the hope that the creation itself also shall be delivered from the bondage of corruption into the glorious liberty of the sons of God.*" We have no true measure of these sad scenes and experiences of earth—and they are sad enough, nothing is to be gained by painting them as lighter than they are; but we can measure them fairly when we get up into the higher region, strong in faith, and share the thought and hope of God. *We are saved by hope.* Let us bless God for it, for the blessed and boundless future in which the far-off interest of tears will be our eternal portion, and the harvest of brave endurance and patient pain. "*Behold we count them patient which endure.*" And who are they? The world's weaklings and fools. Listen to the bead-roll, and hush your moans for very shame. Abel, Enoch, Noah head the line; Abraham, Isaac, Jacob. "*These all died in faith, not having received the promises, but having seen them afar off, and were persuaded of them, and embraced them, and confessed that they were strangers and pilgrims on the earth. For they that say such things declare plainly that they seek a country. And truly, if they had been mindful of that country from whence they came out, they might have had opportunity to have returned. But now they desire a better country, that is an heavenly: wherefore God is not ashamed to be called their God: for he hath prepared for them a city.*" (Heb. xi. 13–16.) "*And what shall I more say? for the time would fail me to tell of Gedeon, and of Barak, and of Samson, and of Jephthae; of David also, and Samuel, and of the prophets: who through faith subdued kingdoms, wrought righteousness, obtained promises, stopped the mouths of lions, quenched the violence of fire, escaped the edge of the sword, out of weakness were made strong, waxed valiant in fight, turned to flight the armies of the aliens. Women received their dead raised to life again: and others were tortured, not accepting deliverance; that they might obtain a better resurrection: and others had trial of cruel mockings and scourgings, yea, moreover of bonds and imprisonment; they were stoned, they were sawn asunder, were tempted, were slain with the sword: they wandered about in sheepskins and goatskins; being destitute, afflicted, tormented; (of whom the world was not worthy:) they wandered in deserts, and in mountains, and in dens and caves of the earth.*" (Heb. xi. 32–38.) "*And these all*"—the world's chief heroes, whose names are dear and honoured through the ages on earth, as they shine resplendent as the stars in heaven's firmament on high—"*These all, having obtained a good report through faith, received not the promise; God having provided some better thing for us, that they without us should not be made perfect.*" (Heb. xi. 39, 40.) "Wherefore seeing ye are compassed about with so great a crowd of witnesses"—these grand and glorious forms, who watch your battles from their thrones, and prepare to hail your triumphant entrance to the kingdom which the victory of faith shall win—"*lay aside every weight, and the sin which doth so easily beset you, and run with patience the race that is set before you, looking unto Jesus the author and finisher of our faith; who for the joy that was set before him endured the cross, despising the shame, and is set down at the right hand of the throne of God.*" (Heb. xii. 1, 2.)

IX.

THE LAW OF ABSTINENCE.

"Wherefore, if meat (food) make my brother to offend, I will eat no flesh while the world standeth, lest I make my brother to offend."—1 Cor. viii. 13.

Of all the great writers of the world, the apostle Paul perhaps most needs to be read with the eye of the heart, as well as with the eye of the understanding. Moral sympathy is an essential condition of the full understanding of the apostle's words. Most especially is it needed in such passages as the present, in which he gives vehement and even passionate utterance to his vivid sympathies with the weaker brethren who were still struggling with the difficulties and perplexities from which his powerful genius had already emancipated him, or who were tormented by doubts which he had laid happily at rest for ever. There is no great writer who is less careful to guard himself from even grave misconstructions, or whose eager, impetuous sentences, when matters which touch his sympathies and affections are in question, are more likely, if formulated into maxims and rules of action, to lead weak minds astray. Indeed, there is a sense in which the Bible is the most unguarded of all books. Meant more than any other book to be a guide of action, it is less careful about misunderstandings of its meaning, and lays itself open to more complete misapprehensions, than any other book in the world. And this precisely because it will be read with the spirit as well as with the understanding. It needs no worldly scholarship; but it will not make its meanings plain to those who do not care to bring to bear on it, not the attention of their heads only, but that of their hearts. How many startling sentences are there which, in the first flash of their meaning, seem to strike at the root of institutions or principles which we learn from other passages the Bible is most earnestly solicitous to maintain and secure. Take some utterances of the mind of the apostle Paul about women for instance, as isolated dicta; treat them as complete authoritative utterances, giving the law to us; the result would be the utter confusion of all man's most sacred relations, and the overthrow of human society. There are words too, uttered by yet more sacred lips, which it needs no little spiritual experience and insight to avoid misunderstanding, and applying to uses which the whole tenour of the Saviour's life and teaching would sternly condemn. Paul, a man vividly sympathetic and tender, easily touched by suffering, easily drawn by love, intense, passionate, and impetuous, suffers himself ever and anon to express in one short, startling sentence some vivid impression which for the moment occupied his whole soul. But we must pause—as he would have paused, nay, did manifestly pause—before we treat it as a mould in which we are to cast our rules of action or habits of life. The sentence expresses the desire and purpose of the apostle's heart, that which would animate and give aim to all its action; but the action itself would be wisely modulated by a hundred secondary considerations, and by other co-ordinate principles, so as to secure, as far as might be possible, the end at which he aimed, without imperilling other and it might be yet higher things. It would be a grand mistake then to formulate such a sentence as this into a rigid rule of action. Treated thus, the first thing which would fall under condemnation would probably be the apostle's life.

These words are very constantly employed as though they laid down a rule of action concerning things indifferent which might lead easily to sin, and set before us a way of helping men against vicious habits at the cost of some personal self-sacrifice. That may be a very important subject, and it has plenty of passages bearing on it in the word of God. But it is not the difficulty here. This passage has quite a different bearing. It is a case, not of a weak will, but of a weak judgment, a weak conscience, in which there is danger of false beliefs or of a lowering of the tone of the conscientious principle of action. It is this, and not any question of vicious habits, which draws from the apostle, who had fought his way through the whole jungle of doubts and difficulties and perplexities in which the weaker brethren were struggling painfully still, these ardent and decisive words.

I. At the root of this declaration lies the conviction that there is no consideration which may compete in a man's motives with the desire to promote the spiritual welfare and progress of mankind. It is the object dearest to God. It was the object dearest to the apostle's heart. It seemed so great to God, so essentially glorious, that God came forth in the form of a man to die for it. This is the true form of the Calvinistic tenet that to God His own glory is His highest end. And Paul was prepared to die for it too. "*And as we tarried there many days, there came down from Judæa a certain prophet, named Agabus. And when he was come unto us, he took Paul's girdle, and bound his own hands and feet, and said, Thus saith the Holy Ghost, So shall the Jews at Jerusalem bind the man that owneth this girdle, and shall deliver him into the hands of the Gentiles. And when we heard these things, both we, and they of that place, besought him not to go up to Jerusalem. Then Paul answered, What mean ye to weep and to break mine heart? for I am ready not to be bound only, but also to die at Jerusalem for the name of the Lord Jesus.*" (Acts xxi. 10–13.) When a man has settled that, and has taken his life in his hand to fulfil a ministry to mankind, he has but one supreme consideration; his own interests vanish; man's interests, the estate of the poorest and most wretched of mankind, fill the sphere of his aims and hopes. (1 Cor. iv. 9–13.) No wonder that nothing could move him from this ministry, and that life was valueless save as it might be a "*finishing his course with joy, and the ministry which he had received of the Lord Jesus to testify the gospel of the grace of God.*" Of course, if life was freely laid on that altar, "*as the life is more than meat, and the body than raiment,*" meats would be freely offered as a sacrifice too. The man who was ready to die for man was not likely to suffer a morsel of meat, any worldly possession, any physical or mental pleasure, to stand for an instant in the way of any help or guidance which he might offer to the weakest of mankind. "*For though I be free from all men, yet have I made myself servant unto all, that I might gain the more. And unto the Jews I became as a Jew, that I might gain the Jews; to them that are under the law, as under the law, that I might gain them that are under the law; to them that are without law, as without law, (being not without law to God, but under the law to Christ,) that I might gain them that are without law. To the weak became I as weak, that I might gain the weak: I am made all things to all men, that I might by all means save some. And this I do for the gospel's sake, that I might be partaker thereof with you.*" (1 Cor. ix. 19–23.) We must take this sentence then, as explaining the full readiness of the apostle, as far as his own tastes, habits, and appetites were concerned, to eat no meat to his dying day, if he saw that such a course of action would remove effectually an offence, a stone of stumbling, from the path of the weakest of his fellow-men.

But all are not apostles. How far is the conduct of this great Christian teacher to be regarded as giving the rule to us? This is but another form of a yet graver question—How far do we feel ourselves bound to be followers of the Son of man in the regeneration, in the reconstruction of man's nature and of human society, in the working out of His benign plans and purposes for mankind? "*Be ye followers of me,*" said Paul, "*as I am of Christ.*" The apostle's life was simply the most Christlike life, and those who care to follow Christ must drink of the same springs, and aim at the same ends, while they pursue the various callings by which society is sustained and developed. To be Christian is to have in us the same mind which was likewise in Christ Jesus. The measure of our Christian vitality is the measure in which that mind is in us, and in which we are able thereby to enter into this language of the apostle Paul. Those that can enter into it perfectly, and can live it, following Paul as Paul followed Christ, are the heaven-sent leaders and ministers of mankind. It is a sacred line which God keeps unbroken through all the ages, the men of apostolic spirit and self-devotion to the good of their fellows. But those who follow can only follow through sympathy. They must be able to believe in this spirit, to make it the aim of their lives to work it out in their limited spheres, with feebler it may be, but with honest and manly effort; or Christianity becomes simply the efflorescence of civilization, and the sad world has to seek its helper, teacher, and saviour still. Clearly then Paul was ready for this, and far more than this, if thereby he might effectually help a weak brother on his way.

II. Actually, as far as we have the means—and we have some means—of knowing, Paul continued to eat meat to his dying day, while the difficulty still remained a pressing one, and the stone of stumbling still continued to block many a weak Christian's path.

What was the difficulty? How did the offence arise? The meat spoken of here is meat which had been offered in an idolatrous temple, and which might be supposed by those who had not the lofty intelligence of the apostle to have contracted some moral contamination thereby. Under all systems the meat offered in sacrifice was in some measure the perquisite of the priest. (Lev. vii. 7–19.) The abuse of the custom is thus described:—"*Now the sons of Eli were sons of Belial; they knew not the Lord. And the priest's custom with the people was, that, when any man offered sacrifice, the priest's servant came, while the flesh was in seething, with a flesh-hook of three teeth in his hand; and he struck it into the pan, or kettle, or caldron, or pot: all that the flesh-hook brought up, the priest took for himself. So they did in Shiloh unto all the Israelites that came thither. Also before they burnt the fat, the priest's servant came, and said to the man that sacrificed, Give flesh to roast for the priest; for he will not have sodden flesh of thee, but raw. And if any man said unto him, Let them not fail to burn the fat presently, and then take as much as thy soul desireth; then he would answer him, Nay; but thou shalt give it me now; and if not I will take it by force. Wherefore the sin of the young men was very great before the Lord: for men abhorred the offering of the Lord."* (1 Sam. ii. 12–17.) There is a very interesting question behind this, into which I must not enter here; how far all animal sacrifice is to be regarded as the consecration of food; the recognition of God as the giver, as the lord of the animal slain, and of man's right to slay as a right which had been delegated by the Lord. That there is some deeper idea in animal sacrifice no thoughtful reader of the Bible, I imagine, can well question; but that this is a very important part of the meaning I feel well assured. It casts a flood of light on the immense slaughter of victims at the consecration of the temple and other high occasions; while it is itself illustrated by the customs of orientals with reference to the slaughter of animals to this day. But the priest's portion was a recognised thing. Portions of this, not needed by the priest's household, would be sold in the shambles. Portions belonging to those who offered the sacrifice might be similarly exposed. Sometimes a feast would be made in the temple, the animal which furnished the flesh being sacrificed there (ver. 10); sometimes in a private house (x. 27), where Christians, following the liberal law, the law of liberty laid down by the apostle (1 Cor. v. 9, 10), would be constantly brought into contact with it, and through it, it might seem to them, with the idol by whose name it had been consecrated. A serious difficulty would thus arise. I beg you to mark carefully where the real heart of the difficulty lay. It was not at all a question of meat in itself, noxious in quality or becoming noxious by quantity. If it had been a question of a man eating unwholesome food, or eating good food to excess, damaging health of body and mind thereby, I cannot imagine that Paul would have treated it as a difficult question at all. You have a sinful habit he would say, you are injuring and destroying your system; you must break it, absolutely, decisively, or perish: what help I can give you as man to man, by the influence of my words or works, is at your service; but it is no question of what I do or do not: it is a simple point, it is between you and God; fly to Him for grace and strength, and master your lust.

But here the case is quite different. It is a case not of a vicious habit, but of a puzzled conscience; a feeble apprehension of truth, a doubt as to what is right or wrong, in which the conduct of the wise and enlightened would be a most wholesome and valuable guide. This weak soul trying to see its way needed guidance. What a glutton or a sot needs is power. For the one use, example is most precious; the other need can only be supplied from a yet deeper spring. How far am I in contact with idolatry in this eating of meat offered to idols? might easily be a very fair question; and not only with the weakest of the young Gentile Church. Some would eat it with conscience of the idol. They would be pained and distressed, and a constant tolerance of such pain and distress is demoralizing. Doing great acts of life with a half heart, with a troubled faith, paralyses conscience, and in the end opens the way to tremendous sins. The constant converse with idolatry which attending these feasts with a "conscience of the idol" would generate, might easily end in apostasy, shipwreck of faith and hope for ever.

How beautiful is the mingled wisdom and charity with which the apostle handles the difficulty! It was absolutely none to him. The idol to him was not anything at all. It was a vain imagination of man's vain heart.

There could be no conscience of an idol in his mind in dealing with anything created by God, however the idol might have been connected with it by others. Who would recognise an usurper because he occupies the palace and assumes the signet of the rightful king? "*The earth is the Lord's, and the fulness thereof.*" The creature is the Lord's, every limb, every particle. If I can but use it for the end for which the Lord created it and put it under my hand, I will rejoice and give thanks that so far the usurper is despoiled. Thus the instructed Jew would look at the matter: "*the idol is not anything at all.*" But the Corinthians were converted Gentiles. The idol was a reality, and a very terrible reality to them; in memory and association at any rate, if not in conviction. Relapse into idolatry, which was all round them, many dear to them being devoted to it, was a very pressing peril; and association with idolaters, with conscience of the idol in the act of association, might easily bring the danger near.

There was but one thing which could deliver them; a thoroughly Christian conviction that the idol is not anything at all: that "*every creature of God is good and is to be received with thanksgiving, being sanctified by the word of God and by prayer.*" But these noble and lofty beliefs are not born in a moment. God had been for ages educating the Jews to the belief of which the Christian Paul, the Hebrew of the Hebrews, in this as in other things was reaping the fruit. And education is a slow and delicate process, and needs to be managed by a nursing hand. While these Gentile converts are being trained to this loftier view, beware lest, puffed up by your superior knowledge, your conduct tempts them to a course which will deaden that fine tact of conscience, by which alone, when it has fastened on the higher truth, the emancipation can be gained. Act on your higher knowledge as your rule of living. The fools and the weaklings are not to be the lords of life and the masters of the world. But if you see any attempt made to draw you into visible contact with the idol, that those weaker than you, led by your example, may be drawn into a contact which to them would be detrimental and degrading, bend the higher law for the moment, or rather lift it higher still—lose it in the lovelier law of charity, and practise a forbearance the motive of which is a brother's good. "*All things are lawful for me, but all things are not expedient: all things are lawful for me, but all things edify not. Let no man seek his own, but every man another's wealth. Whatsoever is sold in the shambles, that eat, asking no question for conscience sake; for the earth is the Lord's, and the fulness thereof. If any of them that believe not bid you to a feast, and ye be disposed to go; whatsoever is set before you, eat, asking no question for conscience sake. But if any man say unto you, This is offered in sacrifice unto idols, eat not for his sake that shewed it, and for conscience sake: for the earth is the Lord's and the fulness thereof: conscience, I say, not thine own, but of the other: for why is my liberty judged of another man's conscience? For if I by grace be a partaker, why am I evil spoken of for that for which I give thanks? Whether ye eat, or drink, or whatsoever ye do, do all to the glory of God.*" (1 Cor. x. 23–31.)

Free use of all God's good gifts with bold conscience is to be the law of Christian living, the daily practice and habit of the life. Voluntary abstinence, forbearance in the use of the freedom, is demanded of us by a yet higher law, the law of Christian charity, the charity which has Christ for its model and inspiration; but only when we find that it will be helpful to a weak brother in our personal intercourse with and influence over his soul. That Paul did not adopt this as his rule of living seems quite indisputable. He could not have omitted to refer to it and explain it in such a passage as 1 Tim. iv. 1–5, if his own rule had been abstinence. "*Now the Spirit speaketh expressly, that in the latter times some shall depart from the faith, giving heed to seducing spirits, and doctrines of devils; speaking lies in hypocrisy; having their conscience seared with a hot iron; forbidding to marry, and commanding to abstain from meats, which God hath created to be received with thanksgiving of them which believe and know the truth. For every creature of God is good, and nothing to be refused, if it be received with thanksgiving; for it is sanctified by the word of God and prayer.*" At the same time we cannot question that he frequently acted on it when brought into personal contact with brethren of weak faith and tender conscience, whom he sought, by sympathy with their doubts and difficulties, to educate to a more vigorous and healthy life. In order to understand what we have every reason to believe was the habit of the apostle's life, the free and temperate use of all the good gifts of God, we must consider—

III. That the adoption of a rule of abstinence, in permanent deference to weak consciences, would simply transfer to the weak the regulation of the order of human life and the progress of the world. The pace of progress would thus be permanently adjusted to the strength of the weakest, instead of being so regulated as to stimulate and help the weaker to press on into the front line. The result would be a grievous impoverishment of moral and mental power; and Christianity, instead of being the power of God unto salvation, would be the instrument of decline and a ministry of death. Surely it is a fundamental principle that the framework of a man's life, his daily habits, should be set in the measure of his own personal stature and power. What suits his character and life, and ministers to his development, he is to embody in his habits, as the best service which he can render to God and to his fellow-men. To be strong, wise, self-controlled, is the best beginning, the only true beginning of real service to mankind. The best work which a man can work at, for the service of his fellows, is his life. To regulate permanent habits on the wants and the weaknesses of others is to deny this principle, and to exalt the influence of spasmodic effort above the broad, grand ministry of life. Paul was far from such illusions.

Freedom was with him the fundamental condition of vital progress; and if his sympathy with the weak and perplexed led him again and again to veil his freedom for the moment, it was that he might help the weak to strength, the perplexed to clearness of vision, the bondsmen to liberty—strength, clearness, and freedom of which he offered conspicuous examples in his own constant habits of life. "Be ye as I am," was his appeal: free and strong; able to see the Lord's mark on all things and creatures, and not the idol's. To live habitually as if he saw the idol's mark would have seemed to him a base act of treason, a shameful forsaking of that liberty which he had in Christ, and which he was resolved to hold for himself and his brethren even unto death.

To generalize and formalize into laws of action the impulses and purposes which inspire the spirit in its personal contact with the will, the consciences, and the affections of its fellows, is in most cases to rob charity of its life and grace of its power. It is to substitute law for grace in our personal relations and dealings with mankind. Had Paul laid down the rule,—There are weak consciences, which cannot get rid of the savour of the idol; they shall rule our conduct; I will never eat meat offered to idols, and I ordain the same to the Church,—the development of mankind by Christianity would have been killed at the very root. Scruples would have become the consecrated thing instead of liberty, and Christianity would have made manifest the weakness of man, instead of the power of God, to the world. No! his supreme concern was that they might master their weakness, break their bonds, and grow from babes to men. If this abstaining from flesh while the world stood would have helped them to that progress, he loved them well enough to do it without a pang of regret. But he evidently was eager to see them rise out of the lower region which is haunted and tormented by such scruples. He ignored them as far as possible, though he dealt with them in tender charity, when, as in chap. x. 28, they were forced on his sight.

Something very parallel to this difficulty of the meat offered to idols was the question about the theatre which was a sore perplexity to pious but intelligent spirits a few years ago. There was something, which had in it essentially no element of evil. But it was closely connected with a world and a worldly life which those nurtured in the Church or brought under its influence were sedulously taught to shun. Many who felt themselves strong abstained. They saw no harm, and would get no harm, but rather a positive good. But they denied themselves, that others of weaker faith might not be in the way of harm, and that no sin or ruin of a brother might by any chance be laid at their door. Whether the rule of abstinence was wise I am not called here to consider. It was complicated by moral considerations—which too were not absent in the case which the apostle treats of here—which make it less easy to pronounce judgment in a word. But it must always be remembered that a rule or law of abstinence in such cases on the part of the strong consecrates the scruple, associates evil permanently with that which has no essential evil in it, and multiplies thereby the stumbling-blocks of mankind.

The case of actual vice, like drinking to excess, seems to me to fall under quite another category; though it is constantly regarded as settled by the text, as though it had been written, "Wherefore, if drink make my brother to offend I will drink no wine while the world standeth, lest I make my brother to offend." We have no call here to discuss and pass judgment on a movement by which men of most unquestioned goodness, and self-devotion to the best interests of others, think that they see a means of largely helping the morally weak by removing a fatal temptation from their path. We only say that it is a question well worthy of the most careful consideration, how far in the long run and on a large scale a permanent confession of weakness can be helpful to human development; how far a habit of life confessedly built on the weakness of others can offer a noble and inspiring example to those who it is hoped would profit by it; and how far an unnatural condition can have in it the elements of a true and vital reformation. But these considerations are really beside the true scope of the text, though they are naturally suggested by it. And in closing this discussion of a perplexed and difficult subject I would say in brief:—(1) That isolated acts of abstinence, which may have their special reason and justification, when moulded into habits fall in the way of the withering denunciation which the passage I have quoted from 1 Tim. iv. 1–4 expresses; (2) That the moulding of our personal habits on the follies, weaknesses, or vices of others, is a betrayal of trust, for that which we have chiefly in trust is life—to live a life free, strong, and fearless, shining as a light, not of rebuke or of caution, but of guidance to mankind; and (3) That every concession to doubt and weakness to which Divine charity moves us is futile and vicious, unless in the very act we are putting forth a hand to lift a weak brother to a standing ground where he will be above these fogs of fear and infirmity for ever.

Butler & Tanner, The Selwood Printing Works, Frome, and London.

www.ingramcontent.com/pod-product-compliance
Lightning Source LLC
LaVergne TN
LVHW021413110826
845150LV00007B/1911

* 9 7 8 1 4 2 5 5 1 0 3 3 6 *